The Making of a Christian Soldier

The Making of a Christian Soldier

L.A. Gomez Jr.

XULON PRESS

Xulon Press
2301 Lucien Way #415
Maitland, FL 32751
407.339.4217
www.xulonpress.com

Copyright © 2019 by L.A. Gomez Jr.

All rights reserved solely by the author. The author guarantees all contents are original and do not infringe upon the legal rights of any other person or work. No part of this book may be reproduced in any form without the permission of the author. The views expressed in this book are not necessarily those of the publisher.

Unless otherwise indicated, all Scriptures are taken from the New King James Version (NKJV) Scripture taken from the New King James Version®. Copyright © 1982 by Thomas Nelson. Used by permission. All rights reserved.

Scriptures marked NLV are taken from the New Life Version (NLV) Copyright © 1969 by Christian Literature International.

Scriptures marked NLT are taken from the New Living Translation (NLT) Holy Bible, New Living Translation, copyright © 1996, 2004, 2007, 2013, 2015 by Tyndale House Foundation. Used by permission of Tyndale House Publishers Inc., Carol Stream, Illinois 60188. All rights reserved.

Scripture quotations marked (NIV) are taken from the Holy Bible, New International Version®, NIV®. Copyright © 1973, 1978, 1984, 2011 by Biblica, Inc.™ Used by permission of Zondervan. All rights reserved worldwide. www.zondervan.com The "NIV" and "New International Version" are trademarks registered in the United States Patent and Trademark Office by Biblica, Inc.™

Edited by Xulon Press.

Printed in the United States of America.

ISBN-13: 978-1-5456-8137-4

DEDICATION

To my wife, three girls, and my dad and mom.

Acknowledgments

First, I'd like to humbly thank my Lord and Savior Jesus Christ for giving me this opportunity to share this experience and comparison that You placed in my heart.

I'd also like to thank my lovely wife, Elva, for being that Proverbs 31 wife. You are truly a blessing from God. Thank you.

Thanks to my three beautiful and wonderful daughters. Ondrea, Jamiliah, and Selena. You are all true blessings from God. I could not have asked for a better set of children. Always remember 3 John 1:4.

I am so grateful to my dad and mom, Leslie and Lucy Gomez, Sr. You have been not only my parents but my pastors, counselors, and friends. I was truly blessed to have you as my parents. You not only taught us the Word of God, but you were examples to me and my brothers, Gee and David.

My gratitude to Dr. Elmer Towns who, in one of my first classes at Liberty University, inspired me to pursue this book to completion.

To all my family and friends who also encouraged me to follow through with this book…Thank you.

TABLE OF CONTENTS

Dedication vii
Acknowledgments ix
Preface xiii
Introduction xv

Chapter 1 – I Shall Fear No Evil 1
Chapter 2 – Getting Recruited 7
Chapter 3 – Arriving at Parris Island Boot Camp 13
Chapter 4 – Going Through the Lord's Boot Camp 19
Chapter 5 – What Happens After Boot Camp? 25
Chapter 6 – Professional Military Education (PME) 31
Chapter 7 – Ready for War 37
Chapter 8 – Enemy Tactics Defeating You 43
Chapter 9 – Treason/Mutiny 49
Chapter 10 – Declare War on the Enemies of God 53
Chapter 11 – Strategic Offensive Principle of War 59
Chapter 12 – "Senior Enlisted" 65

Conclusion – You Are a Prayer Warrior! 71
About the Author 121

PREFACE

A year before I started writing this book, I faced a spiritual crisis. As a spiritual leader, I was always giving and pouring myself into ministry and serving others. Serving Christ and others depletes all of us as Christians. As we pour out great amounts of energy—body, soul, and spirit—we risk being drained, emptied, and overdrawn. At that time, I experienced a spiritual drought as in a wilderness where I felt alone, abandoned, and deserted. I asked myself, "Where are my brothers and sister at arms?"

As a Marine, I knew if I were wounded my fellow combatants would never abandon me; they would be by my side. One of the well-known Marine mottos is:

No man left behind.

That caused me to ask:

- *As Christian soldiers, shouldn't we also protect, help, and support one another when we are in spiritual, relational, and financial battles?*
- *The scriptures tell us we need the armor of God and we are to fight the good fight. Are we not always in warfare?*
- *When other Christians are in trouble, shouldn't our reaction be as "first responders" coming immediately to their aid?*
- *As soldiers of Christ, is there a way for the church to train us for battle?*

The training we go through in the Marines is planned to prepare us for battle and to take care of our fellow comrades. Every disciple should be trained to fight spiritual battles and to restore our fellow brothers and sisters in the Lord. When any Christian faces a new challenge or crisis in life, he or she needs the support, wisdom, prayers, and wise counsel of their fellow warriors.

So I set out to write down for others what I learned from my wilderness...my battlefield experience.

-Pastor Leslie A. Gomez Jr.

INTRODUCTION

The sun set, paving the way for a night of bright stars. A sight to gaze upon undoubtedly. A time for rest and reassurance of a new day that was to come. Although the night was without hesitation, the sound barrier was broken. It was a sound I am not fond of, but there was no time to wonder about that. I must be quick on my feet, tactical in my thoughts, and prepared in my actions. There it went again! The sound burst through the night with no remorse.

My mind flashed back to a more embracing time when the nights were more accepting. When there was no desperation and no worries about what tomorrow may bring, for living within the moment was granting enough.

This moment, on the other hand, was less predictable and scary. I donned my armor and prepared the artillery. My new support system was now a Flak jacket, Kevlar, a Rifle, and a round in the chamber that would travel in my preferred direction.

This was a war zone. Baghdad to be exact. Streets bearing little recognition of peace. We followed the path through Baghdad keeping poised. Our minds, though unspoken, were filled with concern wondering how fate would play out.

What would become of us before the break of day? Every step was a strategic one. We had to think before any movement because there was no room for error. The quality of life came in the form of defense in this environment. There was no turning back and no avoidance.

We were assigned the mission of defending freedom. Within the fine print came the understanding that sacrifice would be a part of that mission. Knowing how or when was never calculated. Could the sound we heard be a marking point of our lives ceasing to see another day?

There was an enemy just as prepared and ready to eliminate us without hesitation. Our objective was to make our way through the city in an orderly maneuver, all the while hoping that we could survive another day.

Our confidence was short-lived as an enemy sniper gained way. At an intersection, the sniper honed in on our point man and took his shot. It happened fast and with no warning. We had seconds to quantify our next move.

It was a moment of realization. We depended highly on our artillery, training, and brotherhood. We stood by our fellowmen without regard to our own lives. The sound we heard was the sound of war, but the rhythm we paced was that of determined practice.

I was no longer just the "Average Joe." Rather I was a Marine committed to the cause of Freedom. I stood for something defined by selflessness. That was me, Gunnery Sergeant Gomez.

It was not just an identification to respond by. It was a structured command development. One that instilled perseverance of unity.

As a Gunnery Sergeant, the very lives of the troops were mine to guard. I embraced them like my own. I never went without these men of great honor. In all honesty, they were more than troops. They had become family.

Introduction

As with any family, my decisions were made in value of our lives. Not one was considered disposable or was disregarded. I wanted to experience the safe return home for each one.

The same ideals came in return. This new-found family was properly trained. They too would sacrifice their own lives to save that of another. Whatever the enemy's plan, it became of no concern for the best who stood by me. From gathering the proper intelligence to making sound decisions, my fellowmen wore an armor both mentally and physically.

We understood that we would be challenged to great lengths and the basis of our training would come in handy. We faced the enemy with selflessness because we were READY!

There is a common saying in the Marine Corps, "Pain is weakness leaving the body." It fits well in many ways, but the one takeaway is that no pain can conquer the COURAGE instilled. Courage is not just a word to define a purpose for a cause or sacrifice. Beyond its definition, it is an act of overcoming an obstacle while present in fear.

This is what makes a Marine. Most importantly, it is how Marines preserve freedom. There is more to the cause than just a single mission. Lives are put in unthinkable situations far from the norm to fulfill those missions.

We each made a conscious decision to serve our beloved country. With that, we also made a **commitment** to our fellow men and women in uniform. A commitment to support and lay down our lives for one another.

Don't let the sacrifice go without notice. "All gave some, and some gave all." All this while facing fear. Could you imagine a commitment so great? It is a direct reflection of the Marine Corps Core Values of Honor, Courage, and Commitment.

The relationship between a military soldier and a Christian soldier should have no differences. As we train our soldiers for war, we must also train Christians to be prepared for the spiritual war that is before us every day. There are disciplines we must insert in our lives to defend and fight for our country, and there are disciplines that we adhere to as well to stay prepared and fit for the spiritual war all around us.

Not every American, and it's even safe to say not every soldier, will ever be face to face in a battle or war against an enemy. However, every Christian will have to face our common enemy, Satan, and all his followers. Though the training needed may be different for different people at different times, it is always to draw us closer to the Lord. As Paul said in 2 Corinthians 12:9-11, it's in our weakness we are the strongest as we are totally dependent on God.

We know how the soldiers of the United States train to be ready for war even if they won't go into battle. Yet we also know every Christian will face battles in their lives, but not every Christian is trained and prepared to face such battles.

Come with me on a journey to discover how a soldier for Christ is the same.

You therefore must endure hardship as a good soldier of Jesus Christ.
No one engaged in warfare entangles himself with the affairs of this life,
that he may please him who enlisted him as a soldier.
(2 Timothy 2:3-4)

Chapter 1
I SHALL FEAR NO EVIL

Proper training prepares a soldier to face any fear and be ready to encounter any danger. I'm a soldier in the United States Marine Corps, but I am also a soldier in the Lord's army. The difference: we train our Marines from the start that everything we do is learning how to fight and survive against our enemy. We are taught this from the very beginning in boot camp. We are always training for war. We are always training for any situation that may arise, knowing that the enemy can attack any one of us at any given moment, and as soldiers, we must be ready.

Churches should and must also provide training for every Christian soldier in order to have a strong army for the Lord. It should begin with "boot camp" style training for our newly enlisted soldiers in the Lord's army. Training new converts to the Lord prepares them for that moment when the enemy attacks. As soldiers, we learn strategic maneuvers and how to identify any unnatural settings in our surroundings to identify an ambush. Our young Christian brothers and sisters, the Lord's elite soldiers, also need to identify and be on the alert watching for the enemy's ambush. They need to know how to identify traps and have situational awareness by knowing their surroundings at all times and being aware of the constant spiritual battle around them.

Training will keep us always alert in our spiritual mindset, knowing the enemy may attack at any moment, in any part of our life, using anyone or anything around us. This requires an awareness in the physical of what it would feel like walking in the midst of a war, and spiritual attention knowing we are walking in the midst of a spiritual war.

A military soldier trains his thoughts, feelings, and attitude as if in a war environment. Our mental state is that we are in the battle. We train as if we are looking forward to going into battle to put the training into practice. The Marines try to instill in every Marine an awareness of our surroundings and to always be on the alert. We need to be of the mindset that no matter what the situation, we look at everything as a weapon of opportunity. Never become complacent, always take different routes especially in foreign countries, travel in pairs or in groups, and be mindful of what we speak in public. The Few, the Proud, the Marines is the mindset after graduating boot camp. There is no arrogance, but we are proud of what we've accomplished and the team or brotherhood that we are now a part of.

A Christian Soldier understands John 16:33 which states, "In the world you will have tribulation." Yet, we are most often surprised by attacks of the enemy. Why aren't we ready? Why are our thoughts so nonchalant? As Christians, we don't associate the spiritual attacks by who they are from, but by who we see in front of us. Romans 12:2 reminds us, "Do not conform to the pattern of this world, but be transformed by the renewing of your mind." Our mindset needs to be focused on the fact that at any time we can and will be attacked. Looking at our surroundings, always on the alert, and being careful what type of environment we put ourselves into keeps us prepared for whatever the enemy will throw at us.

Sometimes, it feels as if Christians are afraid to speak up and say they are Christians or followers of Jesus. The New Life Translation of the Bible says it best in Matthew 10:33, "But whoever does not make Me known in front of men and acts as if he does not know Me, I will not make him known to My Father in heaven." As Christians, we should want to walk proud in the Lord. Denying Christ is not only verbalizing it, but acting the way the world acts is denying Christ as well. If we could only see Jesus' face as Peter did when he denied Christ, we would also weep bitterly.

Being complacent in the spiritual is just as dangerous as becoming complacent in a war zone. As we remember the story of David, he was always in the midst of the battle. He even won just about every battle he was in. The one time he decided to stay at home when his men went into battle was when David saw Bathsheba, and we know the rest of the story. If David had been in battle with his men, he wouldn't have had idle time on his hands to get into trouble. If we are not involved and committed to and working in the local church, we will become idle, and that is when the enemy will hit us with temptations and we will fall.

If we do not realize we are falling, we will continue to fall into deeper waters of sin just like David. The attacks become more consistent and more inviting to the flesh simply because we are not feeding the spirit. We do not have enough clarity to first identify the sin as it is approaching. Secondly, we do not have the willpower spiritually to avoid it or not give heed to it. Paul explained it this way, "What I want to do, I don't and what I don't want to do, I do" (Romans 7:15-20, paraphrase).

The connection between the physical and the spiritual is that we often go by what we see, instead of what we should be believing.

Ephesians 6:12 says, "For our battle is not against flesh and blood, but against the rulers, against the authorities, against the world powers of this darkness, against the spiritual forces of evil in the heavens. (HCSB)" Since we do not physically see it, we tend to not be ready for spiritual battle. When we train and see the threats and our opposing enemies physically, we tend to train harder and be better prepared, even if we never go to battle.

Ask Yourself...

Have I been surprised by an enemy attack?
Why wasn't I prepared?
What is my mindset concerning spiritual warfare?

Action Steps

As a soldier in the Lord's army, it is time to begin conscious training. Training will keep you alert, knowing the enemy may attack at any moment, in any part of your life, using anyone or anything around you. This requires an awareness of both the physical and spiritual world around you.

The Marines try to instill in every Marine an awareness of their surroundings and to always be on the alert.

Christians also need to be of the mindset that no matter what the situation, everything is a weapon of opportunity for your enemy.

Never become complacent.

Look at your surroundings.

Always be on the alert.

Be careful what type of environment you put yourself into.

For we do not wrestle against flesh and blood, but against principalities, against powers, against the rulers of the darkness of this age, against spiritual hosts of wickedness in the heavenly places.(Ephesians 6:12)

Pray and ask God to reveal these enemy forces to you and give you spiritual discernment and alertness.

Chapter 2
GETTING RECRUITED

When I first went to the Marine recruiter's office to join the Marine Corps, I was so excited that nothing or no one could discourage me. There was nothing that was going to stand in my way to become one of the elite: "The Few, The Proud, The Marines." When many friends and acquaintances found out that I was joining the Marine Corps, they all shared their opinions, some good and many not so good.

Some were very encouraging and made me feel as if what I was about to do was something spectacular, something great, something honorable. They supported my decision to become a Marine. On the other hand, many tried to discourage me by saying I would not make it, the Marine Corps would break me, or they talked negatively about the Marine Corps itself. At first, I thought that they cared about me and my safety. After further conversation, I learned that many of them were never in the Marines nor had they ever served in any branch of service. Were they looking out for my best interest, or were they actually envious of something they were afraid to go through with?

As I thought of what and how I needed to train to fit the Marine Corps standards, I began some initial training. I would run around the block, and on a good day I would run around the block twice. I would get on the ground and do push-ups. When I got to twenty-five, I would get up and start looking at my biceps and chest and feel my muscles swelling. I could literally feel my heartbeat and the blood flowing through my veins. I was already seeing myself as a top performer in physical training.

One month prior to leaving for boot camp, my recruiter called me to perform an Initial Strength Test (IST) at 10 a.m. on a Saturday. I figured I had this in the bag. I woke up early Saturday morning and put on my sweatpants and sweatshirt as my mother made me some of her famous buttery French toast, smothered in hot, Aunt Jemima's rich maple syrup, with bacon and scrambled eggs on the side. I had a tall glass of orange juice to wash it down. I was ready to go do this little Initial Strength Test.

My dad drove me to the recruiter's office. I mean who would want to take the bus after this filling meal? I had to conserve my energy for the run around the block, or so I thought. To my surprise, we were timed in a one-and-a-half–Mile run, and tested on twenty pull-ups and eighty sit-ups in two minutes. Well, I was only able to pull myself over the bar for a whopping three pull-ups, couldn't count how many sit-ups I was able to do before I was feeling the effects of all the French toast, but the worst was the mile and a half that seemed like an eternity, tasting orange juice and syrup at the back of my throat the whole way.

After this experience, I started to question if I was making the correct decision for my life. Could I ever really get into shape to hold the title of a United States Marine?

Getting Evangelized

The same holds true when you first come to serve the Lord. After accepting the Lord as your personal Savior, you are so excited about this new life you are about to encounter, and you feel that nothing or no one can discourage you.

Your excitement with your first love towards God has you attending as many services you can attend. You are willing to go and spread this great news, and nothing matters but serving God with all your heart. Many family members and friends may encourage you to continue to serve God. They know and understand this new life you're about to live is better than your life in the world.

At the same time, many of your friends who are still in the world may speak out and try to discourage you about this new thing in your life. It may be that deep down inside they have always wanted to serve God but were scared to. They may have wanted to experience this new love and new life. Maybe they are just being envious because they never did for one reason or another. In any case, they may talk the gospel down or try to discourage this way of living. However, keep searching and you will find out they may have never served the Lord or enjoyed the joy of salvation.

If I had listened to these so-called friends, I would have never joined the Marine Corps. I might never have left Brooklyn, N.Y., which makes me wonder if I would have met my lovely wife and had my three beautiful daughters. I may never have been able to accomplish the things I have accomplished in my life. I would not have been able to travel the world four times. Most importantly, I would not have truly understood what it was to give my life to the Lord, understood the authority of Christ in my life, or what it means to serve and honor the Lord.

Prior to boot camp, I thought the Initial Strength Test would be a breeze. I had done some minimal preparation and training, and I thought that would make me a top performer. So the day of the test, I laced up my sneakers and stretched a bit, but as we started with our pull-ups and sit-ups, reality started to set in. I was not in the greatest shape of my life and quickly learned that once around the block only equals about a quarter of a mile. I also quickly learned that French toast, syrup, eggs, bacon, and orange juice are not an athlete's best friend before any type of intense physical exercise. Needless to say, I failed the initial strength test. Most of all I was embarrassed. I found myself afraid of going to boot camp and failing as many people said I would.

When we first come to Christ, we think we are invincible. One of the first scriptures we learn is Philippians 4:13, "I can do all things through Christ who strengthens me."

Ask Yourself...

- *What happened when you faced your first persecution after coming to Christ?*

- *What happened when you realized you were not really as invincible as you thought you were?*

- *Were you tempted to give up?*

- *Or did you seek to train so that you would not fail the next test?*

Action Steps

Explain what it means to truly give your life to the Lord. If you have not done so, today is the day to make that life-changing decision.

How would you explain the authority of Christ in your life to your family and friends?

How would you describe what it means to serve and honor the Lord with your life?

Would others say you serve and honor the Lord with your life?

It's time to make a life-changing decision, because what you decide will have a ripple effect on the rest of your life and on those you love as well.

Chapter 3

ARRIVING AT PARRIS ISLAND BOOT CAMP

As I left New York to go to Parris Island, I can remember getting on the plane and having a good time joking with the other six guys who left at the same time. We landed in Savannah, Georgia, at about 2200 (10:00 p.m.) and waited for a few more flights to land. When there were about forty of us, they loaded us on a dark bus to head out to Boot Camp. On the drive to Parris Island the jokes became less, it got quiet, then a stillness came over us. That is when I realized a certain fear hit my body, known as *the fear of the unknown*. As we drove into the gates of Marine Corps Recruit Depot, Parris Island (Boot Camp) the driver of the bus told us to close our eyes and put our heads down. All I could think about was, what in the world did I get into?

As the bus stopped, the doors flew open and the Drill Instructor (DI) came aboard. This "Tazmanian devil" was spinning, jumping, and shouting, "Get off my bus! Get on the yellow footprints now! Get off my bus! Get off my bus!" We were definitely not in Kansas anymore as we went through a process called "Receiving."

When you responded to an altar call, your first few minutes, days or weeks as a Christian may have felt the same. Perhaps the fear of the unknown hit you as you hesitated to go before the preacher during the altar call. You may have asked yourself, "If I go up there, what in the world will I be getting into?"

Maybe you felt the conviction so powerful in your life that you accepted the Lord with no hesitation, but then days later you wanted to get back into your routine bad habits. Then you thought and felt, "I shouldn't because that's wrong." Maybe that is where your fear hit, when you thought of what you would have to give up or what you would have to stop doing that was worldly or sinful.

We can relate to this with the Israelites in the book of Exodus. As they left Egypt, they were dancing and rejoicing to be set free. However as time went on, we read that they continued to want to go back to Egypt. They remembered the food and other good things there, conveniently forgetting that they had been slaves. Spiritually speaking, Egypt is the world and receiving Christ as our Lord and Savior frees us from the bondage of sin. We rejoice in this freedom. After a while, though, some remember their Egypt and desires start to grow in their hearts. Unfortunately, some do return to Egypt and some wander in the desert for the rest of their "saved" lives, murmuring, complaining, and never getting to experience the Promised Land here on earth. Blessed are those who choose to believe as Caleb and Joshua did and have crossed over from the Jordan to the Promised Land. They are truly experiencing the joy of their salvation.

Back to my story, I was in "Receiving," where they literally stripped us of all that we owned. The receiving DIs documented and registered us upon arrival in boot camp, then they ordered us to empty all our pockets. Anything personal found in our pockets other than money was considered contraband and thrown in a wastebasket. Then we were marched to another room and given a sea-bag (big green duffle bag) and six sets of everything from underwear to socks to uniforms. Then to another room where we were stripped of all our clothing, which went into a paper bag that was stored in a warehouse until graduation. We put on our new uniforms.

Next we were marched to the Recruit PX and told to pick up every single item on a list they gave us. This list was not optional. They did not ask if you enjoyed the scent of Irish Spring or if Brut 33 aftershave was your favorite. We picked up exactly what was on that list and kept the line moving. Next, we went straight into line for the barbershop.

I was a little uneasy as I had just gotten a fresh-looking fade from my barber back home in New York that cost me almost $20. I thought maybe I would simply get a touch-up. I even looked to see if they had a haircut chart. To my surprise, the barber yelled, "Next!" and before I had a chance to say what style of haircut I wanted, all my hair was shaved off. I felt my grape (head). I had no type of hairstyle, no sideburns, and no fade; I was completely bald.

After all of us were dressed the same and all our faces and heads were shaved, we grabbed our moonbeams (flashlights) and went to the chow hall (dining facility) to get chow (food). We thought we could order the eggs just like we wanted them. Sorry, we all received the same meal of scrambled eggs, bacon, bread, oatmeal, cereal, milk, and OJ. I was sitting there with a bunch of guys from all over the United States, all with the same haircut, the same clothing, and the same clean-shaven face and head. What we did not realize is the Marine Corps was stripping us of any type of individual identity to build us up as a team as "The Few, The Proud, The Marines."

Newly converted Christians should have a similar process. Not that we must shave their heads and dress them all the same, but as leaders in the church we need to teach and instruct new believers which identities of the world should be stripped from their lives. Instead of issuing uniforms and backpacks, we should issue them a Bible, study books, and materials to get them started. Paul says, "Therefore, if anyone is in Christ, he is a new creation; old things have passed away; behold, all things have become new" (2 Corinthians 5:17).

Church leaders need to provide stepping-stones to ease new believers into the deeper things of God that will enhance the transformation of their lives. For far too long we, the leaders of the church, have allowed the younger Christians to continue to live their lives the same. When we finally get around to teaching them why it's important to allow God to transform us, it is a bit more difficult. A small twig, while still young, can be bent to the extent of creating a 360° circle. Once this twig matures and hardens, if you try to bend it, at a certain point will break. Things that must change as Christians are our vocabulary, our way of walk, our thoughts, and our friends to name a few.

As we follow Christ, changes should come from a heart overflowing with God's love and grace. The fruit of the Spirit should become evident in our lives. "But the fruit of the Spirit is love, joy, peace, longsuffering, kindness, goodness, faithfulness, gentleness, self-control" (Galatians 5:22-23).

Instead of the baggy jeans down to their knees, or the miniskirts above their thighs and revealing shirts, we need to explain and educate them how and why they should dress appropriately and modestly. I understand that just dressing the part does not make you a Christian, just as putting on a motorcycle jacket would not make me a biker. However, I am a firm believer that our behavior reflects the way we dress. Just observe people in a restaurant. The ones dressed in jeans eat differently than those wearing a suit.

Many researchers also show that even your mood is directly affected by your clothing. Studies have shown that people who spend an abundance of time dressed in baggy, frumpy clothing tend to feel more depressed, whereas those who wear nicer clothing, such as higher quality tops and jeans, tend to feel happier. (Read more about this at www.SpiritualBridge.com).

This is not only limited to the way we dress, but also the way we behave, the way we speak, our attitudes and our day to day integrity.

As Christians, we represent Christ and we should dress and act as children of Royalty. "But you are a chosen generation, a royal priesthood, a holy nation, His own special people, that you may proclaim the praises of Him who called you out of darkness into His marvelous light" (1 Peter 2:9). If there are dress codes to go to court, school, and weddings, why not wear something that represents us going to the house of God? The Bible is clear that we are ambassadors for Christ. An ambassador is a direct representative of the country he is representing. These ambassadors are the closest person anyone from that country will compare to the president, king or queen of that perspective country. The world views us as a direct reflection of Jesus Christ, and we are to represent the kingdom of heaven to them.

And do not be conformed to this world, but be transformed by the renewing of your mind, that you may prove what is that good and acceptable and perfect will of God. (Romans 12:2)

Ask Yourself...

- *When did my fear of the unknown hit? How did I handle my fear?*

- *Was it when I thought of what I would have to give up?*

- *Was it when I thought about what my friends and family would say?*

- *Has my lifestyle changed since I started following Jesus?*

Action Steps

Things that must change as Christians are our vocabulary, our way of walk, our thoughts, and our friends to name a few. Evaluate how the Fruit of the Spirit is evident in your life. Consider where you need to make some changes so you no longer conform to the world.

Chapter 4

GOING THROUGH THE LORD'S BOOT CAMP

As Christian Soldiers joining and preparing to fight in the Lord's army, we should go through a process of tearing down and reconstruction, a process I want to call the Lord's Boot Camp. It includes dealing with the *fear of the unknown,* of not knowing what is to come in our lives. We must close our eyes, put our heads down, and thank God for what we just got into, knowing we will one day be able to inherit heaven.

As leaders, we must teach young recruits, "Trust in the Lord with all your heart and lean not on your own understanding. Acknowledge Him in all your ways, and He shall direct your paths" (Proverbs 3:5-6). As Christian Drill Instructors, we must also strip them of their worldly individuality and equip them for a fresh start with a new mindset (Ephesians 4:12), a new way of thinking, a new way of living, knowing each Christian is becoming a new person as a new creation in Christ.

Equipping a new Christian includes instructing them to put on the armor of God, to pray, and do spiritual warfare. Ephesians 6:10-18 commands, "Put on the armor of God." So start by giving them the sword - a Bible. Issue them their "uniform" and teach them the meaning of every piece of garment girded with truth, remind them of their helmet of salvation, fit their breastplate of righteousness, then shod their feet with peace, and above all teach them how to use the shield of faith.

Then feed them the bread of Life (John 6), not the world's fast food they want. Explain how we are now the temple of God as it says in 1 Corinthians 3:16. "Do you not know that you are the temple of God and that the Spirit of God dwells in you?" We must start by teaching and discipling new believers about how important it is to respect themselves and their bodies where our Lord dwells. The consequences are all too clear. God refuses to dwell in a temple full and contaminated with sin (1 Corinthians 3:17).

Our first week of boot camp, we were taught how to walk, march, shave, wear our uniforms, Marine Corps orders, general orders, how we must present ourselves, the do's and the don'ts, and all the rules and regulations. This was done by repeating these phrases daily and going over them, over and over again until we literally were saying them in our sleep. We were also told when to go to sleep, when to wake up, and what and when we would eat. That first week was definitely "culture shock." It had to be done the first week. It would not have been effective if it was done two months later or a week prior to graduation.

While new converts are still in their first love or have just gotten on the bus, they are more prone and acceptable to going through the Christian Boot Camp. That is when leaders should disciple them how to become soldiers for the Lord. A new Christian must learn:

- What to eat spiritually, when, how, and why to wake up in the early mornings in order to be in fasting and prayer.
- How to put on the whole armor of God daily, why it's necessary, and what each piece of the armor does, and what the armament of Christ means.

- Why it's necessary for a soldier to wear a uniform and have all their war gear with them at all times. Most importantly, they learn how and when to use it.

Many recruits made it to boot camp, but they did not all graduate. Some could not take the initial change, finding any and every excuse to get sent home. Some couldn't pass the various challenges of the physical fitness test (PFT) or qualify on the rifle range. Not mastering the rifle would get you dropped. In other words, many wanted with all their heart to be a United States Marine but were not able to complete boot camp.

A Christian may begin his/her walk with Christ with great zeal. However, it's not how you start but how you finish that counts. Paul writes, "Do you not know that those who run in a race all run, but one receives the prize? Run in such a way that you may obtain **it**. And everyone who competes **for the prize** is temperate in all things. Now they **do it** to obtain a perishable crown, but we **for** an imperishable **crown**" (1 Corinthians 9:24-25, emphasis added).

I have observed that many Christians are lost for not mastering their sword, the Word of God. But praise God we were called, and we have with us someone who can and will help us qualify, pass boot camp, and win wars. At the end we can say as Paul said, "I have fought the good fight, I have finished the race, I have kept the faith. Finally, there is laid up for me the crown of righteousness, which the Lord, the righteous Judge, will give to me on that Day, and not to me only but also to all who have loved His appearing" (2 Timothy 4:7-8).

You may have heard of many that have come to Christ, but for one reason or another have backslid or simply turned their lives back to their old ways prior to giving their life to Christ. I will not go into whether or not they were ever saved or not, but

Christian leaders are responsible for discipling new believers and raising them up to be leaders who then birth more leaders. We must be that Drill Instructor doing all we can to teach and train them to become successful soldiers for the Lord and eventually graduate and gain the victory into heaven.

In the upcoming chapters, all of that will be explained in more detail. During the first few months of a newly converted Christian's spiritual walk, it is also critical to instill the do's and don'ts, the doctrines and basic teachings of the gospel. Teach and preach truth to them until they can repeat these foundational principles in their sleep. This begins to renew their minds, change their negative attitudes, and develop new patterns of behavior that bless God and others instead of hurting others. Why is it so critical to get them to practice this from the beginning? Try to convince a Christian who has been going to church for years to wake up early to pray and read the Bible daily for two or three hours, after being comfortable in reading the scriptures just on Sundays. It is like the old saying, "It's hard to teach an old dog new tricks." Many Christians have their own concept of what it is to be in the Lord's army, yet they may have never served one day in either army. Let's move forward in discovering how to equip the soldiers in God's army.

Before our deployment to Kuwait, we had to go through extensive NBC (Nuclear Biological Chemical) training. Intelligence predicted this was the enemy's weapon of choice, so we constantly trained to put on our gear and the gas mask, how to take it off if it became contaminated, how to change into new gear if we had to wear it a long period of time, and how to change the filters. Then we would train inside the gas chamber. We were simulating real life scenarios in a controlled environment. Of course, not everyone would take this seriously. You could tell which ones were simply going through the motions because they never believed they would actually need this training in real life.

During our deployment to Kuwait, we were told we were going to be in harm's way and we needed to always carry and have at the ready at minimum our gas masks, but to have our NBC suit readily available. Every week, we would have simulated drills and everyone had to put on their gear and get to the nearest bunker and wait for further instructions. One day the alarm went off, but it wasn't the drill alarm. It was the actual alarm, and we were under attack. Many had their gear close by and put it on, but you could see a few who weren't prepared and panicked to the point they could not get their trousers on right, forgot to put the mask on before the jacket, etc. When the all clear was given, one particular Marine came to me and asked how and why I didn't panic. My reply was, first, I trust in God and secondly, all the training we did kicked in as second nature.

As I thought about this Marine's question and the other situation, it hit me how the Lord prepares us for battles, temptations, and tribulations. However when they hit us, we react unprepared as if we didn't know we could possibly be attacked by the enemy. We forget to adapt, adjust, and overcome these various unexpected trials we face. Sometimes we are looking for the same exact outcome we previously experienced or saw someone else go through, when the reality is that we each have our own battles to fight. Beginning with just trusting in the Lord makes all the difference.

Ask Yourself...

- *Do I trust in the Lord with all my heart and lean not to my own understanding?*

- *Do I acknowledge Him in all my ways, knowing He will direct my paths?*

- *Do I understand and use the armor of God as described in Ephesians 6:10-18?*

- *Do I treat my body as the temple of God?*

Action Steps for Christian Leaders

Equipping a new Christian includes teaching them about the armor of God and how to pray and do spiritual warfare.

Start by giving them the sword, the Bible.

Issue them their uniform and teach them the meaning of every piece of garment and how they are girded with truth. Remind them of their helmet of salvation, show them how to fit their breastplate of righteousness in place, shod their feet with peace, and above all how to use the shield of faith.

Then feed them the correct food, the Bread of Life (read John 6), not the world's fast food they want.

Explain how they are now the temple of God and to respect themselves and their bodies where our Lord dwells.

Chapter 5

WHAT HAPPENS AFTER BOOT CAMP?

Before joining the Marine Corps or going to boot camp, we all took a series of tests (ASVAB) to see what job or in what field, (MOS Military Occupation Specialty) we would be better suited to work. The ASVAB is broken down into Mechanical Comprehension, Assembling Objects, Arithmetic Reasoning, Mathematics Knowledge, Shop Information, Electronics Information, Paragraph Comprehension, Word Knowledge, and General Science. Our skill strengths would determine the type of job we would be eligible for. Even though some may qualify for certain jobs, if there is no opening for that job they must select another job or wait until there is a position available. Some people roll the dice and come in as open contract, meaning after they graduate boot camp they are then told which job position they will be filling.

Every MOS leader wishes to have more Marines in their department to lighten the load. They feel they would be more proficient when in fact, that would make the Marine Corps out of balance. If we overflowed the cooking area, we would have many servers and no one in line to eat the food.

As leaders, we should also be able to discern the gifts or the potential of Christians to try to place them in the work best suited for them. We have so many who feel that the only calling is to be a pastor or worship leader. To lighten the load in our churches, we tend to just add more people to a position, versus seeing the qualifications in the people and then placing them where they are best suited. If the entire congregation were to join the choir, the church would be singing to a bunch of empty chairs with no one to seat the visitors as they arrive. When we get an overflow in one area in the church, other areas and other ministries suffer.

Some may say they love to worship. When they are on the altar, I notice they sing and minister and encourage people to raise their hands and so forth. Yet, when they are in the congregation and someone else is leading the worship, they have their hands in their pockets or their arms crossed. That makes me wonder if they love to worship, or do they love to be seen? This holds true for every ministry. If the only time you see them "performing" is when they are in front of the congregation, then that isn't really their calling. A true worshipper will sing and worship from any pew, after church, in their car, and even in the shower. A true preacher will not only share the gospel when he's in the front of the church, but whenever he has someone and anyone by their side.

> *But to each one of us grace was given according to the measure of Christ's gift... And He Himself gave some to be apostles, some prophets, some evangelists, and some pastors and teachers, for the equipping of the saints for the work of ministry, for the edifying of the body of Christ, till we all come to the unity of the faith and of the knowledge of the Son of God, to a perfect man, to the measure of the stature of the fullness of Christ; that we should no longer be children, tossed to and fro*

and carried about with every wind of doctrine, by the trickery of men, in the cunning craftiness of deceitful plotting, but, speaking the truth in love, may grow up in all things into Him who is the head—Christ— from whom the whole body, joined and knit together by what every joint supplies, according to the effective working by which every part does its share, causes growth of the body for the edifying of itself in love. (Ephesians 4:7, 11-16)

We are all called to spread the gospel, but we all have different gifts and mannerisms to be able to accomplish this. As a pastor, I cannot try to duplicate the pastor from down the street because he has a lot of members and think that I would see the same success if I copied everything he does. Just as every evangelist cannot copy Billy Graham's message and his persona and think they would be able to fill stadiums and see crowds come to Christ. We need to reach within ourselves and depend on God for strength and wisdom, not rely on a handbook or try to cookie cut the ministry given to someone else. Each one of us has our own calling in Christ and a specific way God wants us to utilize our gifts and talents. As pastors we have a responsibility to help new disciples find their unique ministry.

All Marine Recruiters go to Recruiting Duty School in San Diego where they learn the basics of how to recruit kids via school visits, phone calls, and face to face. However, once the Recruiters are on the streets, that's when the real training begins. What worked to recruit one kid will not necessarily work to recruit the next kid. They must adapt, adjust, and overcome every single time with each and every individual kid and situation. Some potential recruits need the recruiter to visit them more than others and assist them or assist their parents in giving guidance. Some potential recruits need some assistance in their PT (Physical Training) performance which may require the recruiter to run or do pull-ups with them two or three times a week.

The same holds true with each ministry whether it is evangelizing, pastoring or even teaching. Not everyone will learn at the same rate nor through the same method of teaching. Not every member in the same congregation will accept the gospel the same way. Pastors may need to visit or call certain members more than others and assist them in their daily walk by praying with them in the mornings, reading a passage of Scripture with them, or maybe just a simple text with a Scripture attached to it.

You may be given the gift of preaching, but does that make you a pastor or an evangelist? You may be an introvert and too shy to stand in front of people, but have a gift of sharing the Word individually with a heart of caring. You may be an extrovert who has no problem in speaking to people you may have just met. In either case, God has a place for you to work in His Kingdom.

Whether working for the United States Marine Corps or the Kingdom of God, we are many members within the same body.

Ask Yourself...

- *Do I know my Christian Occupation Specialty?*

- *Have I taken tests to see what occupation I would be best suited to work in?*

- *There are diversities of gifts, but the same Spirit. There are differences of ministries, but the same Lord* (1 Corinthians 12:4-5).

Action Steps for Christian Leaders

But one and the same Spirit works all these things, distributing to each one individually as He wills. For as the body is one and has many members, but all the members of that one body, being many, are one body, so also is Christ. (1 Corinthians 12:11-12)

As a Christian leader, you need to discern the gifts or potential of the Christians you are called to train and oversee and try to place them in the work best suited for them. One of the ways to do this is to have them take spiritual gifting tests which are readily available online. A good resource is *Finding Your Spiritual Gifts* by C. Peter Wagner.

Chapter 6
Professional Military Education (PME)

The Unfolding of Your Words Gives Light

There is a Professional Military Education (PME) Class for each rank in the Marine Corps. PME classes teach you what you ought to be doing and what you need to do to get ahead and be promoted. As you pick up rank and promotions in the Marine Corps, you are required to attend classes, not only to understand the responsibilities and requirements expected from you, but to also start looking ahead towards your next rank and promotion. If you stop striving to get ahead, others will come from behind and get promoted ahead of you. PME is looked at for consideration towards promotion. Even in corporate America, they look at if you have a degree or not and even which degree you have when considering for hire and promotions. One can never think or believe he knows it all, knows enough, or there is nothing else for him to learn.

As technology and the world around us are advancing, we must continue to keep up with the times. The military strategies from the 1950s have changed significantly to those used today due to the lessons learned from the Korean War. Although I am not old enough to tell you first hand the strategy or the equipment used for the Korean War, I was fortunate enough during my Staff Academy PME to listen to some Korean War Veterans speak about their experience. After that class, I appreciated these men who fought not only the military enemies, but also other enemies like cold weather, lack of food, lack of warm clothing, lack of shelter, and health issues. These men saw their fellow Marines die after running from the enemy and sweating. As they stopped to catch their breath, they froze to death.

Today we have what is called an After-Action Report (AAR) to capture what went right and what went wrong during each operation. There were many lessons learned not only in the Korean war, but from every battle and every mission the United States Marines have participated in.

**There is ALWAYS something to learn;
if we close our minds into thinking what we know is all we need to know,
we will NEVER advance.**

PME classes not only enhance and update us on history and strategy, but also in tasks required of our rank. When you go to the Corporal's Course, you are taught to march and drill with rifles inside the platoon formation, or you could be the one holding the platoon rag (flag). Once you go to the Sergeant's Course, you are taught to be a Platoon leader, how to do basic drills in moving the formation of one or more platoons from one place to another. Being promoted to Staff Sergeant, you are expected to become the Platoon Commander and are required to know how to march and lead ceremonial drills with a sword instead of the rifle, for Change of Commands, Post and Relief, and/or Retirement Ceremonies.

Professional Military Education (pme)

As you are promoted, your level of responsibilities increases as well. For example, as a Private First Class or a Lance Corporal, you are a technician, but as you become a Corporal and Sergeant you are expected to know how to perform the job of a technician, to teach those coming in behind you, *and* become a work center supervisor/Collateral Duty Inspector (CDI). Once you become a Staff Sergeant and Gunnery Sergeant, you are in the role of a manager overseeing the entire department, and so forth. With each promotion, you obtain a higher level of responsibilities, which ensures the continuation of the Marine Corps organization to continue the legacy.

Involve Yourself in Biblical Study with other Christians

But you must continue in the things which you have learned and been assured of, knowing from whom you have learned them, and that from childhood you have known the Holy Scriptures, which are able to make you wise for salvation through faith which is in Christ Jesus. All Scripture is given by inspiration of God, and is profitable for doctrine, for reproof, for correction, for instruction in righteousness, that the man of God may be complete, thoroughly equipped for every good work.
(2 Timothy 3:14-17)

As Christians, although it's not mandatory to go to Bible Study, Sunday School, Bible Institute or Seminary for "promotion" per se, it is the only way to grow spiritually. We read in Luke 2:46-52 that Jesus was found in the temple both listening to the leaders and asking them questions, and that He grew in wisdom. The Son of God grew in wisdom. Why do we think we do not need to grow in wisdom and in the favor of God?

Although continual study is voluntary as Christians, we should have enough passion and thirst for God to want to further our knowledge and wisdom in Christ. When we first come to Christ, we need to attend a type of Discipleship Class, an overall basic class on the purpose of baptism, the purpose of attending church faithfully, the purpose and reasoning for tithing, the understanding of the Father, the Son, and the Holy Spirit, the gifts of the Spirit, etc.

Next, we need to follow up with sound Bible Studies on walking with Christ, building our relationship with Christ, biblical marriage, and how to overcome daily oppositions that distract us from serving God and fulfilling His Will in our lives. Then as we start into the next level of a Bible Institute, we learn to grow and are able to minister the Word of God to others. In a Bible Institute, we need to seek out courses or classes in Bible Skills, Ministry Skills, and Life Skills.

Learning to teach, preach, and share the gospel to others fulfills our calling as Christians and a Church. Jesus knew the Word and combatted Satan with the Word, but He had to know the Word in order to do it. Satan opposed Him by twisting the Word, but Jesus knew the correct context and was able to resist.

Satan will confuse you and destroy you, using the Word if you do not know it. The Word of God is your sword for defeating the devices of the enemy (2 Corinthians 2:11).

Have Your Children in SunDay School

Sunday School is on a whole different level. I can say first hand, the things I learned in Sunday school came back to memory in difficult times in my life, especially when I backslid when I first joined the Marine Corps. It is our responsibility as

Christian parents to ensure that our children know about God in order to sustain them. Our children are in the public school system more hours in the week than they are learning the Word of God. We need to be like the parents of Daniel and Joshua, so that even when we are not around our children have enough knowledge and wisdom about God and their faith to stand firm on what they believe.

We see because of Daniel's teachings about God at around the age of twelve, he purposed in his heart that he wouldn't defile himself with the king's delicacies nor with the wine. We also see the reward as God brought Daniel into favor and goodwill even with his enemies.

Although the Bible doesn't mention if Joshua's parents died before leaving Egypt or after, we can see in Joshua's life how he maintained himself before the Lord. Joshua even made it a point to get close to Moses and become his helper because he knew Moses was a man of God. Joshua wanted to avoid being contaminated so he would go with Moses to the tabernacle and stay in the tabernacle even after Moses left.

How sad it was that the entire generation that crossed into the Promised Land were uncertain on who their God was. In Joshua 24:15, Joshua starts off by saying, "If it seems evil to you to serve the Lord." Did you ever ask yourself why Joshua would ask such a thing? It wasn't totally the people's fault as you read that their parents and grandparents were the generations that died in the desert because of the murmuring and complaining against God. All these children heard from their parents were comments like, "God just brought us to the desert to let us die, we have no water, we have no meat, we were better off in Egypt," etc. What child in their right mind would want to serve that God?

So, as children or adults, early in our Christian walk we need to embrace the Word of God to know God and to grow body, mind, and spirit in our relationship with God. This will continue the legacy of the Kingdom of God in our own homes and for future generations. As parents, we want to be able to declare, *"I have no greater joy than to hear that my children walk in truth."* 3 John 1:4

Be diligent to present yourself approved to God, a worker who does not need to be ashamed, rightly dividing the word of truth. (2 Timothy 2:15)

Ask Yourself...

- *As technology and the world around me are advancing, am I keeping up with the times?*

- *Am I a learner for life or have I closed my mind thinking what I know is all I need to know?*

- *As a parent, can I declare, "I have no greater joy than to hear that my children walk in truth"?*

Action Steps

We are learners for life. Self-education in our Christian life starts with daily Bible reading of a chapter or more a day. Take notes. Look up what words mean in Vine's or Strong's or online. Read a Christian book and a business, self-help, history, or biography book each month as well.

Involve yourself in biblical study with other Christians.

Have your children in Sunday School.

Chapter 7

READY FOR WAR

Accountability in the military is one soldier to the other, trying to ensure as many Marines as possible get home from a mission. In the midst of different types of conflicts, you not only concentrate on your own fight, you are also watching over your fellow Marines. Any Marine is vulnerable to being wounded in combat, and some may perish of these life-threatening wounds.

One of the ways to ensure we get home is to know and train with the weapons available to us. There are many weapons we utilize in the Marine Corps. The first weapon we have to master is the rifle, M16A1. It has an effective firing range of 600 yards. It is semi-automatic and can fire a single shot or a three-round burst. The enemy at 600 yards is far enough away that the kill or the potential harm by the enemy is not all that personal. But what happens when the enemy is at arm's reach? Can you or do you utilize the rifle or set it on three round burst?

This is why we learned to use different weapons. At seven to ten yards you would use your 9 MM pistol. If the enemy gets closer than that, you would utilize your bayonet. If that isn't available, you resort to hand to hand combat. In any case at any distance, there is always a weapon available for the fight. If the enemy is a mile away and there are plenty of them, that's when we call in the Big Guns, Infantry Mortar platoon, or call for an Air Support Strike.

The section in Ephesians 6 describes the armor of God we are to use and our weapons. These include praying at all times in the Spirit and being on the alert with all perseverance and petition for all the saints.

As Christians, we are called to be accountable one to another because sins are battle wounds from the enemy, whether Satan, our flesh, our minds, or our deceitful hearts. In other words, we are surrounded by our enemy twenty-four hours a day, seven days a week. No matter how you want to view it, every sin we have committed leaves a scar. A scar is a healed wound. James 5:16 says, "Therefore, confess your sins to one another and pray for one another, that you may be healed. The prayer of a righteous person has great power as it is working."

Although the Bible shows there is no difference in sin before God, we understand that some sins are bigger and stronger than others. Once we confess our sins to the Lord, we receive forgiveness. When we confess our sins one to another, that is the sign we are free, liberated, and healed from that sin. When we hide sin, it's because there is shame and guilt. Our enemy uses shame and guilt to keep us from confessing and ultimately keep us being healed from sin. James goes on to say, "Prayer of a righteous person has great power as it is working." In other words, prayer is a very effective weapon. Jesus gives us a sample in John 17 when He prays for Himself, His disciples, and all believers, past, present, and future. Jesus' prayer in John 17 demonstrates to us the different effective ranges in prayer. Some prayers are general and long distance like for distant relatives, the government, etc. Some prayers are close and personal like when you are fighting for your marriage, your kids, etc.

Two are better than one, because they have a good reward for their toil. For if they fall, one will lift up his fellow. But woe to him who is alone when he falls and has not another to lift him up! (Ecclesiastes 4:9-10)

My brothers, if anyone among you wanders from the truth and someone brings him back, let him know that whoever brings back a sinner from his wandering will save his soul from death and will cover a multitude of sins. (James 5:19-20)

Take care, brothers, lest there be in any of you an evil, unbelieving heart, leading you to fall away from the living God. But exhort one another every day, as long as it is called "today," that none of you may be hardened by the deceitfulness of sin. (Hebrews 3:12-13)

Even if we have our weapons and have mastered them, we can still be wounded. Although we may pray for certain situations, we may still get hurt or wounded. However, we also know the enemy has no power of death over us. His blows might wound us to feel as we'd like to die as Elijah did, but God will not allow a death-striking blow from Satan for us to fall.

There was a song many years ago that said, "Lean on me when you are not strong, and I will help you carry on, for it won't be long, till I'm going to need someone to lean on." In Galatians 6:1, the Bible commands us to exalt, to lift those that are wounded. We must be compassionate toward backslidden or wounded believers who have fallen during an enemy attack so that no soldier is left behind.

In the book of Luke, there was a son who left his father's house and lived a certain period of time in a way that was not pleasing to the father. After spending all his money, he realized his father's servants had it better off than he did. So he thought of how he would go home and ask for forgiveness of his father. The parable states that while he was still a long way off, the father ran to him and restored him. That father represents our Heavenly Father. Yet when he returned to his father's house, his brother had something against him in his heart that he freely expressed. He couldn't accept that his brother was forgiven. I believe he hurt his father's heart more so than that of his little brother when he told his father, "That son of yours." He did not say "my brother" as if he wanted nothing to do with him.

Some Christians have the same reactions to fallen brothers and sisters and feel they do not deserve forgiveness and should die in their sins outside of the father's house. We all sin, just in different ways. As we ask for forgiveness and mercy to God, we **must** learn to extend that same grace to others. The parable of the Unmerciful Servant in Matthew 18:21-35 shows us that our sin debt God has forgiven us for is so much bigger than anything that anyone could do to us. In my observation though, it seems like when we do not want to forgive, it's because we want to make it all about ourselves. Just as the brother of the prodigal son made it about himself, saying all these years "I" have been here, "I" have served you, I, I, I. Until we focus on Jesus and return to a heart for Jesus, we will not have a heart to see the kingdom of heaven expand and have compassion not to want to see souls lost for an eternity in hell. We cannot forget our purpose as Christians or our purpose as a church.

Commander's Intent Strategy

The Commander's Intent may be understood as the overall goal the Commander wants to achieve. He may give five or six sub-goals, but after that it is up to each unit commander under him to plan strategies in keeping with the Commander's Intent. These strategies are given down to the lowest command element always with the Commander's Intent in mind. The Commander cannot micromanage to the smallest detail to the lowest command element. The Commander must have confidence in his unit commanders. The unit commanders must have confidence in their Officers. The Officers must have confidence in their Staff Non-Commissioned Officers. The Staff Non-Commissioned Officers must have confidence in their Enlisted and Junior Marines.

Even if the Unit Commanding Officers do not agree with the top-level Commander, they still press on with the vision or intent of the top Commander. If the lower commanders show that they do not agree with the top Commander, it undermines the top-level Commander. The junior Marines will not respect the orders given to them and will not put 100 percent effort into achieving success. Many Marines could lose their lives because they are not focused.

A Commander can feel like he is being undermined when he states an order and any leadership in between him and the junior troops expresses disagreement with the Commander. The Junior Troops will naturally have more confidence with the leadership closer to them, so if those closer leaders don't support the top Commander, the junior troops will question the orders.

The same holds true for an effective healthy growing church. The doctrines, rules, and vision of the church are led by the Pastor and leaders cannot ignore or dismiss what he or she feels should be followed. During a church leadership meeting, the leadership should feel free to express their options. However, once a rule or an event is finalized by the Pastor, even if a leader did not agree, he should not express his opinion to the members of the church. He should embrace it and pass on to the members what is to be done as if he agreed 100 percent. By expressing his opposite opinion, it causes division. Nine out of ten times, if dissension is sown, whatever plan was passed will not be accomplished or not even given a chance. The enemy loves that because if there was even a twenty-five or thirty percent success, the church would never know it. This also causes much discouragement among the members because to them it seems as the leadership is all talk and no action.

Ask Yourself...

- *Do I effectively use my weapon of praying at all times in the Spirit?*

- *Do I perseverance and petition for all the saints?*

- *Do I confess my sins to the Lord and then to one to another?*

- *Or am I experiencing shame and guilt?*

- *Do I extend forgiveness and grace to fallen brothers and sisters?*

Action Steps for Christian Leaders

The doctrines, rules, and vision of the church are led by the Pastor and leaders cannot ignore or dismiss what he or she feels should be followed.

During the church leadership meeting, express your opinions.

However, once a rule or an event is finalized by the Pastor, even if you did not agree, do not express your opinion to the members.

Chapter 8

ENEMY TACTICS DEFEATING YOU

Be self-controlled and alert. Your enemy the devil prowls around like a roaring lion looking for someone to devour. Resist him, standing firm in the faith. (1 Peter 5:8-9)

The easiest soldier the enemy can kill and destroy is the soldier asleep at his post. In the past, we had what we called foxholes. It was a hole in the ground, deep and wide enough to have two Marines standing up with the rifle at the ready (with magazine inserted and one round in the chamber). We would watch for any movement of the enemy trying to advance, especially in the dark hours. It has been said that during the Vietnam War, if the enemy caught the American soldiers sleeping in their foxholes, they would kill one of them and leave the other sleeping. Once the other would wake up to his fellow Marine dead, that would torment him to the extent he was no good anymore in the fight. Another story told by the Korean Soldiers was that their own Officers would kill them for falling asleep while on Post for putting the rest of their fellow soldiers in danger. A Marine has a serious responsibility for not only his own life, but also for the lives of his fellow soldiers.

Another enemy tactic is stopping the essential supplies from reaching the soldiers. Desert Storm was literally won because the Iraqi soldiers were giving up, turning in their rifles and weapons to the U.S. soldiers in exchange for food. When a soldier faces hunger, there is no willingness to fight. It's believed that when asked, "What a soldier most needs in war?" Napoleon answered, "A full belly and a good pair of shoes."

This brings me to the basic daily supplies that make a difference in "fight or flight." The Korean War, or the Forgotten War as it was called in the '50s, was a war where we learned many valuable lessons, and unfortunately learned them at the cost of many American soldiers' lives. When I attended the Staff Academy, we had a class about the Korean War by Marines who survived and returned home. Their personal experiences were heartbreaking to say the least. One of them had half an ear he said was from frostbite. They told us stories on how many of their fellow soldiers froze to death trying to sleep in the middle of the night. They would have to tuck their MRE's (Meals Ready to Eat) under their armpits to warm them enough in order to eat what they called their food-cycles. They were not fully prepared to fight under those extreme cold conditions.

Ever see a movie where the guys are shooting their guns and never seem to run out of bullets? Well in real life, you are issued just so many bullets. After you run out of bullets, you must return to the ASP (Ammunition Supply Point). Yes, another essential supply is ammunition. Simply put, no bullets, no use of your rifle.

There are five important things in war that the enemy tries to take out:

Supplies: Supplies build morale, such as flack jacket, coats, gloves, and anything that helps you to focus on the war.

Food: No food means no willingness to fight because a soldier will concentrate on hunger pains. During Desert Storm, they were giving up just so they could eat.

Bullets: With no ammunition to fight the enemy, how would you take them down?

Medicine: If you don't heal the wounded they will die. If they catch a stomach virus and spread it to everyone, how can they fight?

Communications: This is the biggest and most important. If your means of communications gets cut off and there is no communication between the soldiers, they could shoot at one another. It can also cause loss of morale and confusion. The commander's intent and vision must be kept before them or it could be forgotten.

The Strategy of the Enemy

Be sober, be vigilant; because your adversary the devil walks about like a roaring lion, seeking whom he may devour. (1 Peter 5:8)

As Christian soldiers, we need to be prepared for the tactics we know our enemy is going to employ against us. We can study how the enemy has come against God's people by reading the accounts in His Word that have been given to us in our "Soldiers' Manual," the Bible. The good soldier knows that the enemy is ever active and never rests. The good soldier knows that the enemy is shrewd and ever attacking, but he also knows the Lord is there to help him. He knows that regardless of the trap, God will make a way of escape for him. The good soldier studies the methods of his enemy and learns his weaknesses. The good Christian soldier needs to be wise to the ways of the devil and he needs to know that the Lord Jesus is greater than any enemy we will ever face (1 John 4:4).

The Bible teaches that Satan has certain methods of operations. Paul writes, "Stand firm against the schemes of the devil" (Ephesians 6:11). The Greek word for "schemes" is *methodia*—the root from which we get our term "methods" or "methodology." Likewise, he writes, "We are not ignorant of [Satan's] schemes" (2 Corinthians 2:11).

Theologian Merrill Unger writes, "Missions involving espionage are frequently as crucial to winning a war as actual battles. Without intelligence of the enemy's strength and position, the results of any military encounter would be highly dubious. Yet believers sometimes display an obvious disinterest in what the Bible reveals about Satan and demons. Or, what is even worse, they manifest a morbid fear of such a study. This apathy or dread is almost as perilous as the opposite extreme of fanatical occupation with evil."[1]

What are Satan's methods against believers?

Start in the Garden of Eden and read the exchange between Eve and the enemy. He disguised himself as something beautiful. 2 Corinthians 11:14 describes him as a beautiful angel of light. Though many of us find snakes to be threatening now, in the Garden of Eden there were no dangers from any of the

---

[1] Unger, Merrill. *What Demons Can Do to Saints*. Moody Publishers: Chicago. 1991.

animals. Satan went on to using deception and perversion of the Word of God to tempt Eve to sin.

It says in Genesis 3:1, "Now the serpent was more cunning than any beast of the field which the Lord had made." Jesus said, "[Satan] was a murderer from the beginning" (John 8:44), and he "comes only to steal and kill and destroy" (John 10:10). The Apostle Paul warns, "But I fear, lest somehow, as the serpent deceived Eve by his craftiness, so your minds may be corrupted from the simplicity that is in Christ."

Characteristics of Satan

1. **Created** by God, but **not equal** to God. (Proverbs 16:4)
2. Defies God and **despises truth.** (John 8:44)
3. Was given **limited power.** (Job 1:8-12)
4. **Commands** a **hierarchy of demons.** (Ephesians 6:10-12)
5. **Masquerades** as "an angel of light." (2 Corinthians 11:14-15)
6. Plans to **steal, kill,** and **destroy.** (John 10:10)
7. **Rules the masses** *outside* **God's protection.** (Ephesians 2:1-3)
8. Keeps seeking an "opportune time" to **tempt** us. (Luke 4:13)
9. Tries to **hide** the actual **truth** about our God. (2 Corinthians 4:3-4)
10. **Offers counterfeit promises** he can›t fulfill. (Genesis 3:4-5)
11. **Twists Scriptures** to fit his purposes. (Genesis 3:1-5 and Luke 4:1-13)
12. Will suffer the fate he deserves. (Revelation 20:10)

Ask Yourself…

- *Do I display a disinterest in what the Bible reveals about Satan and demons?*

- *Do I manifest a morbid fear of such a study?*

- *Has my mind been corrupted from the simplicity that is in Christ by the deception of the enemy's lies?*

Action Steps for Christian Soldiers

We all need to realize we are part of the Army of the Lord. We must be aware of the enemy's tactics. Satan wants to immobilize us and keep us from progressing in our spiritual lives, and therefore, he will come with many different attacks. He wants to keep us from building and completing the work that God has called us to. Because our enemy is both wise and relentless, we must be aware of his tricks and schemes.

Read 2 Corinthians 2:11, 1 Peter 5:8-9, John 10:10, John 8:44, Genesis 3:1, and Ephesians 6:11.

Write down the tactics of your enemy and how to use this information to your advantage.

Chapter 9

TREASON/MUTINY

Treason is a betrayal of the nation, kingdom, or state to which one owes allegiance. It is also a betrayal of trust. Mutiny is conspiracy among a group of people to openly oppose, change, or overthrow a lawful authority to which they are subject. Treason and mutiny are both punishable by death in most societies.

> *But understand this, that in the last days there will come times of difficulty. For people will be lovers of self, lovers of money, proud, arrogant, abusive, disobedient to their parents, ungrateful, unholy, heartless, unappeasable, slanderous, without self-control, brutal, not loving good, treacherous, reckless, swollen with conceit, lovers of pleasure rather than lovers of God.*
> (2 Timothy 3:1-4)

I have witnessed a few church divisions or church splits that occurred because of a member or someone who attended that church did not agree with the authority or found a disagreement with the church or the pastor. This person then started to murmur, complain, and create a stir within the members. Instead of going to the pastor, this person started to get other members on his or her side. These selected few would then get a plan together to start a new "church." They said they were called by God to pastor a church and tried taking all those not in agreement with what was going on in that church.

King David's own son committed such an act of treason against his own father. In 2 Samuel 15–19, we see how Absalom's greed and envy got the best of him. He wanted to overthrow his own father as king, going behind his back and trying to win over the people in David's kingdom. We see David's attitude not only as a father, but as a man of God. He sends word throughout the kingdom to do no harm to his son, Absalom. David's heart was saddened to see his own son not understand how even when David was being persecuted by Saul, David knew not to touch God's anointed. Although God had anointed David as king, and David was in the situation where Saul's life was in his hand, David simply cut a piece of King Saul's robe to show how close he was to him (1 Samuel 24). In fact, David tried to make amends with Saul, even called him father to show he had no animosity towards him. Yet, we see the wicked outcome on the life of Saul for not repenting and forgiving.

This teaches us we need to pray to God that God may change the hearts of those causing or trying to cause division within the church before it's too late and death falls upon them. Absalom suffered a horrific death because of his evil against the kingdom of God. The Word shows us it's God who places and removes kings (Daniel 2:21). God also places and removes pastors. It's not up to man to put in place kings over God's people. It's not man's place or power to place and remove pastors and their ministries.

If the story of Absalom isn't enough, I encourage you to read Numbers 12, where God showed His disapproval to

Miriam and Aaron for speaking out against Moses. They realized their shortcomings and repented before God. Although they repented, we see God still punished them for speaking out against the man He put in the position of leadership.

God calls for the unity of the church, the unity of the believers. In John 17:20–26, we read one of the greatest commandments for the church to be unified. Jesus further states in Matthew 12:25, "Every kingdom divided against itself is brought to desolation, and every city or house divided against itself will not stand." Then in verse 30, Jesus says, "He who is not with Me is against Me, and he who does not gather with Me scatters abroad."

Treason is punishable by death. In Matthew 7:21–23, Jesus said, "Not everyone who says to Me, 'Lord, Lord,' shall enter the kingdom of heaven, but he who does the will of My Father in heaven. Many will say to Me in that day, 'Lord, Lord, have we not prophesied in Your name, cast out demons in Your name, and done many wonders in Your name?' And then I will declare to them, 'I never knew you; depart from Me, you who practice lawlessness!'"

Ask Yourself...

- *How would I define treason against God's kingdom?*

- *Have I caused dissension among other believers that Christ would call inciting a mutiny against His designated leaders?*

Action Steps

Read Matthew 12:25, 12:30, and 7:21–23.

How have these verses opened your eyes to your role as a Christian soldier for Christ?

Are there changes you need to make in your current lifestyle?

Chapter 10

DECLARE WAR ON THE ENEMIES OF GOD

Every place that the sole of your foot will tread upon I have given you, as I said to Moses. From the wilderness and this Lebanon as far as the great river, the River Euphrates, all the land of the Hittites, and to the Great Sea toward the going down of the sun, shall be your territory. No man shall be able to stand before you all the days of your life; as I was with Moses, so I will be with you. I will not leave you nor forsake you. Be strong and of good courage, for to this people you shall divide as an inheritance the land which I swore to their fathers to give them. (Joshua 1:3-6)

On September 16, 2001, just after the attack on September 11, President George W. Bush declared the "War on Terrorism." He deployed thousands of troops to Iraq, Afghanistan, and many other nations to seek out the enemy that had threatened, attacked, destroyed, and killed many people.

A terrorist may be defined as someone who uses violence, intimidation, destroying property, or forceful tactics to get what they want.

Deployed in Enemy Territory

Therefore, prepare your minds for action, keep sober in spirit, fix your hope completely on the grace to be brought to you at the revelation of Jesus Christ.
(1 Peter 1:13)

Unlike a boxer who trains for months for a title bout, a spiritual battle may take you by surprise at any moment. It's more like when I was a kid walking through the streets of New York. You never knew who or what was lurking around the corner. Someone could have accused you of stepping on their sneakers and suddenly wanted to fight you for it.

I checked into my unit in February of 2009 and in March 2009, I was boot on ground in Afghanistan. As Marines, we start by going to Boot Camp, Marine Combat Training, our Academies, and yearly training in order to get and stay prepared for real war life situations. Furthermore, our training didn't focus on individual training; it focused more on unit training, a unit working as one. In the midst of battle, in the midst of war, you must always be mindful that you may have to depend on your fellow Marine. Many may think about the greater things such as fighting with you in your foxhole, but sometimes it may be in the simplest thing. It may be simply someone to talk to when you are feeling some of the fatigues of war, like missing home, or receiving bad news from back home.

In 1 Samuel 17:32, a young David said to King Saul, "Let no one lose heart on account of this Philistine; your servant will go and fight him." David went from a lunch delivery kid to a warrior in a *moment's notice*. What qualified David to fight? Many say it was because he had experience as a shepherd when he fought and killed a lion and a bear. Some say he had mastered the sling-shot in his spare time. Many say it was his trust in God and because Goliath was uncircumcised, he wasn't under the pact of God the way he was. It was a combination of it all those things. We cannot rely on fighting every battle with only one resource. Prayer, Fasting, Worship, Reading the Word, and so forth are all weapons we need to master in order to get and stay trained for real Spiritual Warfare. We never know when the next Spiritual attack will be, so we must always be prepared.

Job was another man who demonstrated what it was to be ready in a moment's notice. We are introduced to Job as a man righteous before God. He not only offered prayers and sacrifices for himself but for his kids in case they fell short before God and didn't know it. When Satan asked God if he could attack Job, God said he could but he had to spare Job's life. Satan did exactly that. Job was attacked in every aspect of his life and lost everything. Yet his spirituality and relationship with God gave him the strength and weapons to stay faithful to God when everything told him to turn away.

In John 16:33 Jesus said, "In this world we will have tribulation." So why do we get offended at God when we go through trials in our lives? Why aren't we confident in the latter part of the verse when Jesus says, "But be of good cheer for I have overcome the world"? If we are in Christ, we should abide in His peace, even in the midst of the storms. The scriptures also tell us to not forsake the assembling of ourselves together. We need to walk together and encourage one another, even for the simplest trials in our lives.

Proverbs 27:17 says, "Iron sharpens iron, So one man sharpens another" (NIV).

Since Boot Camp we are taught accountability, every morning we would hold up our money valuable bags and count off from the first recruit to the last. This let the Drill Instructors know we were all accounted for each morning. We also had to account for every rifle which was done by everyone who had duty during the night known as fire-watch. Fire-watch consisted of two Marines per hour and they would count the rifles and ensure everyone could sleep safe and not have to worry about someone coming in, in the middle of the night and stealing anything. Little did we know this was preparing us for actual war situations where accountability and safekeeping would be crucial for mission success.

During combat, accountability is excelled to one of the highest priorities amongst a few other things. An emphasis I want us to look at more than anything in this chapter is the accountability to fellow Marines. In combat situations Marines must look out for each other and have each other's back 24/7 especially in the darkest hours. If one of my fellow Marines was to get wounded in action, that Marine would expect for me and the rest of us to come back for him or her just as I would expect of them to do if I was to get wounded. No matter how hectic the battle, how many enemies we had around us, or if even it was his own fault he was wounded, our top priority has changed and that is to get him back to safety, and healed.

As Christians, we need to ask ourselves how important is it to me to look out for my fellow brother or sister in Christ. If my brother was wounded by the enemy how far will I go to go after him so he may be rescued or recovered from the hands of the enemy? If he fell in sin, would I have the courage to approach him and speak to him in love and lead him back to repentance? Do I approach him as Jesus approach the situation of the woman caught in adultery or do I fall in the crowd that accused her? If my fellow brother has been wounded or felt betrayed in his walk in Christ by a fellow brother, a Pastor, or a church, would I have the valor to aid him back to health?

Would I aid him as the Samaritan aided the wounded man, or do I act as the Priest or Levite who crossed the street to avoid him?

As Christians, this should give us a new perspective on, "No man left behind". As a Marine expects his fellow Marines to aid him if he has been wounded, God expects us to do the same for those wounded in Spiritual Battle.

Galatians 6:1 Brethren, if a man is overtaken in any trespass, you who are spiritual restore such a one in a spirit of gentleness, considering yourself lest you also be tempted.

Chapter 11

STRATEGIC OFFENSIVE PRINCIPLE OF WAR

In every occasion where I was deployed overseas into a hostile environment, we landed in the middle of the night. During the last minutes of our flight, we would go into "Tactical Blackout." We donned our tactical gear on and held our weapons close by, bright lights would go out on the aircraft, and soft black lights or blue lights came on. We landed in our enemy's territory the most stealthy way possible. The enemy never knew how many aircraft were coming in, how many troops, nor what equipment we had, etc. Although it wasn't a straight-out sneak attack, we did not announce what we were bringing to the battle.

This Strategic Offensive Principle of War has been applied to many fields of endeavor including sports. Simply put it says, "The Best Defense is a Good Offense." Moving forward on the attack keeps the enemy off balance while he tries to fight back and moves backwards. Mao Zedong explained it saying, "Often success rests on destroying the enemy's ability to attack."[2]

This same principle works in our Christian warfare. Psalm 44:5 says, "Through You we will push down our adversaries;

---

[2] www.brainyquote.com/authors/mao_zedong

Through Your name we will trample those who rise up against us."

As Christian Soldiers, we are to get our tactical gear on and keep our weapons close at hand. Ephesians 6:10-18 explains the tactical gear God has provided for us to use in both our defensive and offensive battle against the enemies of God. The Apostle Paul, a man who had been behind enemy lines and was experienced in spiritual warfare, tells us in verse ten, "Be strong in the Lord and in the power of His might." He assures us we have what we need to stand against the tactics of our enemy if we put on all our tactical gear. "Put on the whole armor of God, that you may be able to stand against the wiles of the devil" (verse 11).

Then he describes these enemy forces saying, "For we do not wrestle against flesh and blood, but against principalities, against powers, against the rulers of the darkness of this age, against spiritual hosts of wickedness in the heavenly places." In other words, we are fighting against a well-organized army that consists of **principalities**, from the Greek word *arche* meaning the chief ranking or highest authorities in Satan's forces. Then there are the **powers** who have delegated authority or jurisdiction over certain portions of the earth, and **rulers** who are demonic forces assigned to influence world leaders. Finally, we have the lowest-ranking and most numerous of the satanic forces, **spiritual hosts of wickedness**.

Once again, our experienced "military" instructor tells us we need every piece of our tactical gear, "Therefore take up the whole armor of God, that you may be able to withstand in the evil day, and having done all, to stand" (verse 13). Paul is saying that if we do not have all our tactical gear in place, we will be vulnerable during the upcoming battle. He is also encouraging us that when we have done all we are supposed to do, we will be able to stand against the enemy forces.

This experienced spiritual warrior then describes for us each piece of our tactical gear. No soldier goes into battle without understanding what each piece of his gear is designed to do.

The **helmet of salvation** covers your mind and protects your thoughts. In training Timothy, Paul told him, "No one engaged in warfare entangles himself with the affairs of this life, that he may please him who enlisted him as a soldier" (2 Timothy 2:4). In other words, our thoughts must be focused on Jesus and that will keep the mind-game tactics of the enemy from infiltrating our minds. We need to stay alert and vigilant against our adversary, the devil, who walks around like a roaring lion, seeking whom he may devour (1 Peter 5:8).

The **breastplate of righteousness** covers our heart. In 2 Timothy 2:22, Paul tells Timothy, "Flee youthful lusts, but pursue righteousness." Jesus said, "But seek first the kingdom of God and His righteousness, and all these things shall be added to you" (Matthew 6:33). Do things God's way and He will make sure we have what we need to live in victory, defeating every enemy.

Wear the **belt of truth**. Jesus said, "I am the way, the truth, and the life" (John 14:6). If we have the truth firmly fixed in our mind, we will not be deceived by the lies and tricks of the enemy.

Though a soldier is prepared for war, his goal is to keep the **peace**. Paul tells us to "shod your feet with the preparation of the gospel of peace" (Eph 6:15). Jesus spoke often of giving His disciples His peace, the kind the enemy cannot steal from them no matter what their circumstances (John 14:27).

The **shield of faith** repels the "arrows" the enemy aims at us. They are aimed at our minds trying to cause doubt and fear.

Our faith must be placed in our commander-in-chief. He will lead us to victory.

The Bible is called the **sword of the Spirit**. A sword is meant to block blows as well as to strike in order to wound and kill the enemy. It is a defensive as well as an offensive weapon.

It is time to declare war and return the fight to the very doorstep of what the enemy is trying to destroy in our lives. We are fully equipped with the Armor of God. Let's use it. Furthermore, the Word of God gives us the tools of prayer and fasting over these issues. The Lord has already given us the victory over our adversary.

But thanks be to God, who gives us the victory through our Lord Jesus Christ. (1 Corinthians 15:57)

It's like when God told Moses to send twelve spies to seek out the land He was going to give them, yet ten spies came back looking at the situation of the giants that dwelled in the land (Numbers 13). At no time did God ask them to assess the situation. The battle was already won. He just wanted them to see the spoils that were about to be given to them. What that means to us today is the victory is ours in our marriages, our children, our finances, and everything that God has given us. Everything belongs to the Lord and the battle is already won. He said firmly, "It is finished" (John 19:30). In John 16:33 Jesus assured us, "I have overcome the world."

It is not by our strength or in our own power, but "by My Spirit," says the Lord (Zechariah 4:6). In Psalm 18:39, David tells us, "For You have armed me with strength for the battle; You have subdued under me those who rose up against me."

Ask Yourself...

- *Have I declared war on the enemy that is trying to destroy my marriage, my children, and my finances?*

- *Am I using the armor and the tools God has given me to take back what the enemy has stolen from me?*

- *Am I truly living in victory?*

Action Steps

Read Ephesians 6:10-18.

List the instructions, the armor of God, and how to use each piece given to us in this passage.

Chapter 12
"Senior Enlisted"

Moses took his tent and pitched it outside the camp, far from the camp, and called it the tabernacle of meeting. And it came to pass that everyone who sought the Lord went out to the tabernacle of meeting which was outside the camp. So it was, whenever Moses went out to the tabernacle, that all the people rose, and each man stood at his tent door and watched Moses until he had gone into the tabernacle. And it came to pass, when Moses entered the tabernacle, that the pillar of cloud descended and stood at the door of the tabernacle, and the Lord talked with Moses. All the people saw the pillar of cloud standing at the tabernacle door, and all the people rose and worshiped, each man in his tent door. So the Lord spoke to Moses face to face, as a man speaks to his friend. And he would return to the camp, but his servant Joshua the son of Nun, a young man, did not depart from the tabernacle. (Exodus 33:7-11)

Not much is recorded in the Scriptures about Joshua's parents, whether they died in Egypt or in the desert. In either case, we know they instructed their son in the ways of the Lord because Joshua understood he needed godly guidance, a godly role model, and a godly father figure. We know Joshua was Moses' successor, but he didn't just appear after Moses died. He had walked and learned from Moses.

Joshua was a young kid when he saw the afflictions of his parents and his people in Egypt. He saw miracles take place in Egypt, including the death angel claiming the lives of all the firstborn of the Egyptians. He experienced leaving Egypt with gold and an abundance of God's blessings. He was a young adult as he experienced crossing the desert. He probably heard all the complaining and murmuring going on, but he stood away from that and continued to trust in the Lord. He also experienced the cloud and the fire God provided as protection from the sun in the day and warmth at night.

Joshua was one of the spies who went out with the twelve but came back with good news, unlike the other ten. He and Caleb stood upright in their faith when the others around him were faithless. His trust in the Lord endured the forty years of walking in a circle when others might have said, "We'll catch you in the next go around."

He fought with the army of Israel, then became Commander in Chief. He saw how God responded as Moses' hands were held up while he fought in the battle. He witnessed how God provided food and water from a rock for them. He didn't complain about eating what was provided but gave thanks for the meal.

So in his elder days, Joshua sat down with the people who were the children of all the ones who died in the desert. He told them his lifelong experience with God. He started his statement with, "But if it seems evil to serve the Lord..." Joshua understood that this generation only heard the complaints at home. They heard their parents complaining about no food, no water, making the sarcastic remarks maybe there are no tombs in Egypt and how Moses brought them out there to die.

Their thoughts could have been negative about God, but Joshua shared his experience with this generation. He told what the Lord brought them through and then posed the statement, "But as for me and my house, we will serve the Lord" (Joshua 24:15).

In the New Testament, the Apostle Paul says in 2 Timothy 2:2, "The things which you have heard from me in the presence of many witnesses, entrust these to faithful men who will be able to teach others also." As Christian leaders, we have a responsibility to share our stories of God's faithfulness. Our testimony is another powerful weapon in overcoming the enemy. (Revelation 12:11).

The Marine Corps has what is known as Senior Enlisted. Simply stated, these are the people with all their experience and years in the Marine Corps. They are possibly the ones to make better decisions on improving the Marine Corps or improving some of the rules put in place. Starting at the unit level, the Master Gunnery Sergeant (MGySgt) will have his staff meeting with the Staff Non-Commissioned Officers (SNCO) to make the plans and scheduling for the Department. Next level up, the MGySgt has his weekly meeting with the other MGySgts in the Unit and with the Unit Sergeant Major (SgtMaj) to discuss the plans and scheduling for the entire Unit. The SgtMaj has his weekly meetings with the other SgtMajs from all the other Units on base with the Command SgtMaj to discuss the plans and requirements expected so all the Units are working under the same guidelines. The Command SgtMajs also have their weekly meetings with the Base SgtMaj and the Base SgtMajs have their meetings with the Marine Air Wing Sgt Maj. It continues to trickle up until it reaches the SgtMaj of the Marine Corps which is the highest Enlisted position a SgtMaj may have. Even though payrate wise they are all E-9s, their billet holds a higher position as the Senior Enlisted.

Retirement

Although you may retire from active duty, you can still be called upon for advice. The Joint Chiefs of Staff is composed of Marine, Army, and Navy officials who are well past retirement. The JCS advise the President and are the direct link between the soldiers on the battlefield, Congress, and all those who make decisions that could put our soldiers in harm's way. Although the JCS themselves are not on the battlefield, because of their experience they are looked to for help in keeping our country safe from the enemy, fighting against terrorism, and prioritizing troop movement and placement.

I believe General Colin Powell is one of the best examples. He obtained the rank of a Four-star General and became the twelfth Chairman of the Joint Chiefs of Staff to later become the 65th United States Secretary of State. His experience, knowledge, and training were just a few of the qualifications that earned him those positions. Many Presidents past and present lean on the experiences of the JCS not only for how and what works, but also to learn what didn't work and why. If we do not learn from our past, we are doomed to repeat it.

Although the Israelites repeated history quite of a number of times, they did not on Joshua's watch. Joshua understood, recognized, and shared his position on taking the children of God forward.

> *Israel served the Lord all the days of Joshua, and all the days of the elders who outlived Joshua, who had known all the works of the Lord which He had done for Israel.* (Joshua 24:31)

"senior Enlisted"

You may retire from different, active leadership roles and ministries in the church, but you never retire from being a spiritual soldier and warrior for Christ. What does that mean? Let's turn for a final word on that.

Conclusion

YOU ARE A PRAYER WARRIOR!

For the weapons of our warfare are not carnal but mighty in God for pulling down strongholds, casting down arguments and every high thing that exalts itself against the knowledge of God, bringing every thought into captivity to the obedience of Christ, and being ready to punish all disobedience when your obedience is fulfilled (2 Corinthians 10:4-6).

Soldier of Jesus Christ, pay attention and follow these orders:

Since you are always at war with the enemy of your soul, put on the full armor of God and take up your mightiest spiritual weapon: PRAYER! When you put on His armor, how do you stand firm against the wiles of the devil? You are "praying always with all prayer and supplication in the Spirit, being watchful to this end with all perseverance and supplication for all the saints" (Ephesians 6:18).

When you pray, declare the Word of God, which is the sword of the Spirit! Praying Scripture at all times releases the truth of God into your mind, thus renewing your mind. Your old, past thoughts, feelings and behavioral habits(which are carnal) are replaced by the absolute truth of God. You have the mind of Christ. Your first thought, feeling or action is no longer rooted in your old ways but in your renewed mind. You are not conformed to the world's way of warfare; you are transformed through the renewing of your mind as you pray and obey the Word of God (Romans 12:2).

Never quit praying. Pray without ceasing...pray always with perseverance. Be watchful as you pray. God will speak to you through Scripture, preaching and teaching, dreams, visions, and prophetic words. Henry Blackaby in *Experiencing God* instructs, "We don't choose what we will do for God; He invites us to join Him where He wants to involve us."[3] Stop praying for God to join you in what you are doing; join God in what He is doing. Watch for where He is moving by His Spirit in worship and in the world. Pray for what God wants, not for what you want. Stop trying to get God to agree with you in prayer and start agreeing with Him in prayer.

Every soldier must be trained and equipped in using the spiritual weapons God has given us, not just to fight but to fight the good fight, to run the race, and to finish strong (2 Timothy 4:7). At the end of this book, I have given you a 30-day battle plan for renewing your mind and equipping your prayer life

---

[3] https://www.goodreads.com/author/quotes/21025.Henry_T_Blackaby

to be the prayer warrior God calls you to be. Enlist in His prayer army.

Some Christians say to me, "I don't know how to pray." Really? Jesus taught you how to pray and then commanded you to pray. As a soldier in the military, I was trained to obey what my leaders told me to do. So, are you willing to obey? Every day pray *The Lord's Prayer*.

By the third century A.D., the early church leaders were also praying *The Jesus Prayer* without ceasing. What is that, you ask? Those soldiers for Christ prayed all the time either in their conscious mind or subconscious, "Lord Jesus Christ, Son of God, have mercy on me, a sinner." That renewed their minds along with memorization and meditating on Scripture.

I have taken the early church training manual for the soldiers of Christ, who warred and prayed without ceasing in the spirit, and created for you a **30-Day Prayer Warrior Training Manual**. Use it. Overcome by the blood of the Lamb and the word of your testimony. Pray, see God answer your prayers, and declare your testimony as His soldier that Jesus Christ is surely *The King of kings and Lord of lords!*

30-Day Prayer Warrior Training Manual

This needs a paragraph or two introducing the Didiche and what it is (I've gone to church my whole life and I've never heard of it!). Also introduce *Seventy-Seven Irrefutable Truths of Prayer*. Talk about why you chose these, how you compiled them, any adaptations you made, how to use this manual, etc.

THE DADICHE

The teaching of the Lord to the gentiles by the twelve apostles (also known as the Dadiche)

Translated by J.B. Lightfoot from the Greek. http://housechurch.org/miscellaneous/didiche.html

Day 1

> Dadiche 1:1 There are two ways, one of life and one of death, and there is a great difference between the two ways.
>
> Dadiche 1:2 The way of life is this. First of all, thou shalt love the God that made thee; secondly, Thy neighbor as thyself. And all things whatsoever thou wouldst not have befall thyself, neither do thou unto another.
>
> Dadiche 1:3 Now of these words the doctrine is this. Bless them that curse you, and pray for your enemies and fast for them that persecute you; for what thank is it, if ye love them that love you? Do not even the Gentiles the same? But do ye love them that hate you, and ye shall not have an enemy.
>
> Dadiche 1:4 Abstain thou from fleshly and bodily lusts. If any man give thee a blow on thy right cheek, turn to him the other also, and thou shalt be perfect; If a man impress thee to go with him one mile, go with him twain; if a man take away thy cloak, give him thy coat

also; if a man take away from thee that which is thy own, ask it not back, for neither art thou able.

Dadiche 1:5 To every man that asketh of thee give, and ask not back for the Father desireth that gifts be given to all from His own bounties. Blessed is he that giveth according to the commandment; for he is guiltless. Woe to him that receiveth; for, if a man receiveth having need, he is guiltless; but he that hath no need shall give satisfaction why and wherefore he received and being put in confinement he shall be examined concerning the deeds that he hath done, and he shall not come out thence until he hath given back the last farthing.

Dadiche 1:6 Yea, as touching this also it is said; Let thine alms sweat into thine hands, until thou have learnt to whom to give.

Obey this teaching and repent of your disobedience.

Read Matthew 6. Pray the Lord's Prayer three times and The Jesus Prayer without ceasing.

Day 2

Dadiche 2:1 And this is the second commandment of the teaching.

Dadiche 2:2 Thou shalt do no murder, thou shalt not commit adultery, thou shalt not corrupt boys, thou shalt not commit fornication, thou shalt not steal, thou shalt not deal in magic, thou shalt do no sorcery, thou shalt not murder a child by abortion nor kill them when born, thou shalt not covet thy neighbors goods.

Dadiche 2:3 Thou shalt not perjure thyself, thou shalt not bear false witness, thou shalt not speak evil, thou shalt not cherish a grudge.

Dadiche 2:4 Thou shalt not be double–Minded nor double-tongued; for the double tongue is a snare of death.

Dadiche 2:5 Thy word shall not be false or empty, but fulfilled by action.

Dadiche 2:6 Thou shalt not be avaricious nor a plunderer nor a hypocrite nor ill-tempered nor proud. Thou shalt not entertain an evil design against thy neighbor.

Dadiche 2:7 Thou shalt not hate any man but some thou shalt reprove, and for others thou shalt pray, and others thou shalt love more than thy life.

Obey this teaching and repent of your disobedience.

Read Matthew 6. Pray the Lord's Prayer three times and The Jesus Prayer without ceasing.

Day 3

Dadiche 3:1 My child, flee from every evil and everything that resembleth it.

Dadiche 3:2 Be not angry, for anger leadeth to murder, nor jealous nor contentious nor wrathful; for of all these things murders are engendered.

Dadiche 3:3 My child, be not lustful, for lust leadeth to fornication, neither foul-speaking neither with uplifted eyes; for of all these things adulteries are engendered.

Dadiche 3:4 My child, be no dealer in omens, since it leads to idolatry, nor an enchanter nor an astrologer nor a magician, neither be willing to look at them; for from all these things idolatry is engendered.

Dadiche 3:5 My child, be not a liar, since lying leads to theft, neither avaricious neither vainglorious; for from all these things thefts are engendered.

Dadiche 3:6 My child, be not a murmurer, since it leadeth to blasphemy, neither self-willed neither a thinker of evil thoughts; for from all these things blasphemies are engendered.

Dadiche 3:7 But be meek, since the meek shall inherit the earth.

Dadiche 3:8 Be long-suffering and pitiful and guileless and quiet and kindly and always fearing the words which thou hast heard.

Dadiche 3:9 Thou shalt not exalt thyself, neither shalt thou admit boldness into thy soul. Thy soul shall not cleave together with the lofty, but with the righteous and humble shalt thou walk.

Dadiche 3:10 The accidents that befall thee thou shalt receive as good, knowing that nothing is done without God.

Obey this teaching and repent of your disobedience.

Read Matthew 6. Pray the Lord's Prayer three times and The Jesus Prayer without ceasing.

Day 4

Dadiche 4:1 My child, thou shalt remember him that speaketh unto thee the word of God night and day, and shalt honor him as the Lord; for whencesoever the Lordship speaketh, there is the Lord.

Dadiche 4:2 Moreover thou shalt seek out day by day the persons of the saints, that thou mayest find rest in their words.

Dadiche 4:3 Thou shalt not make a schism, but thou shalt pacify them that contend; thou shalt judge righteously, thou shalt not make a difference in a person to reprove him for transgressions.

Dadiche 4:4 Thou shalt not doubt whether a thing shall be or not be.

Dadiche 4:5 Be not thou found holding out thy hands to receive, but drawing them in as to giving.

Dadiche 4:6 If thou hast ought passing through thy hands, thou shalt give a ransom for thy sins.

Dadiche 4:7 Thou shalt not hesitate to give, neither shalt thou murmur when giving; for thou shalt know who is the good paymaster of thy reward.

Dadiche 4:8 Thou shalt not turn away from him that is in want, but shalt make thy brother partaker in all things, and shalt not say that anything is thy own. For if ye are fellow-partakers in that which is imperishable, how much rather in the things which are perishable.

Dadiche 4:9 Thou shalt not withhold thy hand from thy son or from thy daughter, but from their youth thou shalt teach them the fear of God.

Dadiche 4:10 Thou shalt not command thy bondservant or thine handmaid in thy bitterness who trust in the same God as thyself, lest haply they should cease to fear the God who is over both of you; for He cometh, not to call men with respect of persons, but He cometh to those whom the Spirit hath prepared.

Dadiche 4:11 But ye, servants, shall be subject unto your masters, as to a type of God, in shame and fear.

Dadiche 4:12 Thou shalt hate all hypocrisy, and everything that is not pleasing to the Lord.

Dadiche 4:13 Thou shalt never forsake the commandments of the Lord but shalt keep those things which thou hast received, neither adding to them nor taking away from them.

Dadiche 4:14 In church thou shalt confess thy transgressions, and shalt not betake thyself to prayer with an evil conscience. This is the way of life.

Obey this teaching and repent of your disobedience.

Read Matthew 6. Pray the Lord's Prayer three times and The Jesus Prayer without ceasing.

Day 5

Dadiche 5:1 But the way of death is this. First of all, it is evil and full of a curse; murders, adulteries, lusts, fornications, thefts, idolatries, magical arts, witchcrafts, plunderings, false witnessings, hypocrisies, doubleness of heart, treachery, pride, malice, stubbornness, covetousness, foul - speaking, jealousy, boldness, exaltation, boastfulness.

Dadiche 5:2 Persecutors of good men, hating truth, loving a lie, not perceiving the reward of righteousness, not cleaving to the good nor to righteous judgment, wakeful not for that which is good but for that which is evil-from whom gentleness and forbearance stand aloof; loving vain things, pursuing a recompense, not pitying the poor man, not toiling for him that is oppressed with toil, not recognizing Him that made them, murderers of children, corrupters of the creatures of God, turning away from him that is in want, oppressing him that is afflicted, advocates of the wealthy, unjust judges of the poor, altogether sinful. May ye be delivered, my children, from all these things.

Obey this teaching and repent of your disobedience.

Read Matthew 6. Pray the Lord's Prayer three times and The Jesus Prayer without ceasing.

Day 6

Dadiche 6:1 See lest any man lead you astray from this way of righteousness, for he teacheth thee apart from God.

Dadiche 6:2 For if thou art able to bear the whole yoke of the Lord, thou shalt be perfect; but if thou art not able, do that which thou art able.

Dadiche 6:3 But concerning eating, bear that which thou art able; yet abstain by all means from meat sacrificed to idols; for it is the worship of dead gods.

Obey this teaching and repent of your disobedience.

Read Matthew 6. Pray the Lord's Prayer three times and The Jesus Prayer without ceasing.

Day 7

Dadiche 7:1 But concerning baptism, thus shall ye baptize. Having first recited all these things, baptize in the name of the Father and of the Son and of the Holy Spirit in living (running) water.

Dadiche 7:2 But if thou hast not living water, then baptize in other water; and if thou art not able in cold, then in warm.

Dadiche 7:3 But if thou hast neither, then pour water on the head thrice in the name of the Father and of the Son and of the Holy Spirit.

Dadiche 7:4 But before the baptism let him that baptizeth and him that is baptized fast, and any others also who are able; and thou shalt order him that is baptized to fast a day or two before.

Obey this teaching and repent of your disobedience.

Read Matthew 6. Pray the Lord's Prayer three times and The Jesus Prayer without ceasing.

Day 8

Dadiche 8:1 And let not your fastings be with the hypocrites, for they fast on the second and the fifth day of the week; but do ye keep your fast on the fourth and on the preparation (the sixth) day.

Dadiche 8:2 Neither pray ye as the hypocrites, but as the Lord commanded in His Gospel, thus pray ye: Our Father, which art in heaven, hallowed be Thy name; Thy kingdom come; Thy will be done, as in heaven, so also on earth; give us this day our daily bread; and forgive us our debt, as we forgive our debtors; and lead us not into temptation, but deliver us from the evil one; for Thine is the power and the glory for ever and ever.

Dadiche 8:3 Three times in the day pray ye so.

Obey this teaching and repent of your disobedience.

Read Matthew 6. Pray the Lord's Prayer three times and The Jesus Prayer without ceasing.

Day 9

Dadiche 9:1 But as touching the eucharistic thanksgiving give ye thanks thus.

Dadiche 9:2 First, as regards the cup: We give Thee thanks, O our Father, for the holy vine of Thy son David, which Thou madest known unto us through Thy Son Jesus; Thine is the glory for ever and ever.

Dadiche 9:3 Then as regarding the broken bread: We give Thee thanks, O our Father, for the life and knowledge which Thou didst make known unto us through Thy Son Jesus; Thine is the glory for ever and ever.

Dadiche 9:4 As this broken bread was scattered upon the mountains and being gathered together became one, so may Thy Church be gathered together from the ends of the earth into Thy kingdom; for Thine is the glory and the power through Jesus Christ for ever and ever.

Dadiche 9:5 But let no one eat or drink of this eucharistic thanksgiving, but they that have been baptized into the name of the Lord; for concerning this also the Lord hath said: Give not that which is holy to the dogs.

Obey this teaching and repent of your disobedience.

Read Matthew 6. Pray the Lord's Prayer three times and The Jesus Prayer without ceasing.

Day 10

Dadiche 10:1 And after ye are satisfied thus give ye thanks.

Dadiche 10:2 We give Thee thanks, Holy Father, for Thy holy name, which Thou hast made to tabernacle in our hearts, and for the knowledge and faith and immortality, which Thou hast made known unto us through Thy Son Jesus; Thine is the glory for ever and ever.

Dadiche 10:3 Thou, Almighty Master, didst create all things for Thy name's sake, and didst give food and drink unto men for enjoyment, that they might render thanks to Thee; but didst bestow upon us spiritual food and drink and eternal life through Thy Son.

Dadiche 10:4 Before all things we give Thee thanks that Thou art powerful; Thine is the glory for ever and ever.

Dadiche 10:5 Remember, Lord, Thy Church to deliver it from all evil and to perfect it in Thy love; and gather it together from the four winds - even the Church which has been sanctified - into Thy kingdom which Thou hast prepared for it; for Thine is the power and the glory for ever and ever.

Dadiche 10:6 May grace come and may this world pass away. Hosanna to the God of David. If any man is holy, let him come; if any man is not, let him repent. Maran Atha. Amen.

Dadiche 10:7 But permit the prophets to offer thanksgiving as much as they desire.

Obey this teaching and repent of your disobedience.

Read Matthew 6. Pray the Lord's Prayer three times and The Jesus Prayer without ceasing.

Day 11

Dadiche 11:1 Whosoever therefore shall come and teach you all these things that have been said before, receive him.

Dadiche 11:2 But if the teacher himself be perverted and teach a different doctrine to the destruction thereof, hear him not; but if to the increase of righteousness and the knowledge of the Lord, receive him as the Lord.

Dadiche 11:3 But concerning the apostles and prophets, so do ye according to the ordinance of the Gospel.

Dadiche 11:4 Let every apostle, when he cometh to you, be received as the Lord.

Dadiche 11:5 But he shall not abide more than a single day, or if there be need, a second likewise; but if he abide three days, he is a false prophet.

Dadiche 11:6 And when he departeth let the apostle receive nothing save bread, until he findeth shelter; but if he ask money, he is a false prophet.

Dadiche 11:7 And any prophet speaking in the Spirit ye shall not try neither discern; for every sin shall be forgiven, but this sin shall not be forgiven.

Dadiche 11:8 Yet not every one that speaketh in the Spirit is a prophet, but only if he have the ways of the Lord. From his ways therefore the false prophet and the prophet shall be recognized.

Dadiche 11:9 And no prophet when he ordereth a table in the Spirit shall eat of it; otherwise he is a false prophet.

Dadiche 11:10 And every prophet teaching the truth, if he doeth not what he teacheth, is a false prophet.

Dadiche 11:11 And every prophet approved and found true, if he doeth ought as an outward mystery typical of the Church, and yet teacheth you not to do all that he himself doeth, shall not be judged before you; he hath his judgment in the presence of God; for in like manner also did the prophets of old time.

Dadiche 11:12 And whosoever shall say in the Spirit, Give me silver or anything else, ye shall not listen to him; but if he tell you to give on behalf of others that are in want, let no man judge him.

Obey this teaching and repent of your disobedience.

Read Matthew 6. Pray the Lord's Prayer three times and The Jesus Prayer without ceasing.

Day 12

Dadiche 12:1 But let everyone that cometh in the name of the Lord be received; and then when ye have tested him ye shall know him, for ye shall have understanding on the right hand and on the left.

Dadiche 12:2 If the comer is a traveler, assist him, so far as ye are able; but he shall not stay with you more than two or three days, if it be necessary.

Dadiche 12:3 But if he wishes to settle with you, being a craftsman, let him work for and eat his bread.

Dadiche 12:4 But if he has no craft, according to your wisdom provide how he shall live as a Christian among you, but not in idleness.

Dadiche 12:5 If he will not do this, he is trafficking upon Christ. Beware of such men.

Obey this teaching and repent of your disobedience.

Read Matthew 6. Pray the Lord's Prayer three times and The Jesus Prayer without ceasing.

Day 13

Dadiche 13:1 But every time prophet desiring to settle among you is worthy of his food.

Dadiche 13:2 In like manner a true teacher is also worthy, like the workman, of his food.

Dadiche 13:3 Every firstfruit then of the produce of the wine-vat and of the threshing-floor, of thy oxen and of thy sheep, thou shalt take and give as the firstfruit to the prophets; for they are your chief-priests.

Dadiche 13:4 But if ye have not a prophet, give them to the poor.

Dadiche 13:5 If thou makest bread, take the firstfruit and give according to the commandment.

Dadiche 13:6 In like manner, when thou openest a jar of wine or of oil, take the firstfruit and give to the prophets.

Dadiche 13:7 Yea and of money and raiment and every possession take the firstfruit, as shall seem good to thee, and give according to the commandment.

Obey this teaching and repent of your disobedience.

Read Matthew 6. Pray the Lord's Prayer three times and The Jesus Prayer without ceasing.

Day 14

Dadiche 14:1 And on the Lord's own day gather yourselves together and break bread and give thanks, first confessing your transgressions, that your sacrifice may be pure.

Dadiche 14:2 And let no man, having his dispute with his fellow, join your assembly until they have been reconciled, that your sacrifice may not be defiled.

Dadiche 14:3 For this sacrifice it is that was spoken of by the Lord; In every place and at every time offer me a pure sacrifice; for I am a great king, saith the Lord, and My name is wonderful among the nations.

Obey this teaching and repent of your disobedience.

Read Matthew 6. Pray the Lord's Prayer three times and The Jesus Prayer without ceasing.

Day 15

Dadiche 15:1 Appoint for yourselves therefore bishops and deacons worthy of the Lord, men who are meek and not lovers of money, and true and approved; for unto you they also perform the service of the prophets and teachers.

Dadiche 15:2 Therefore despise them not; for they are your honorable men along with the prophets and teachers.

Dadiche 15:3 And reprove one another, not in anger but in peace, as ye find in the Gospel; and let no one speak to any that has gone wrong towards his neighbor, neither let him hear a word from you, until he repent.

Dadiche 15:4 But your prayers and your almsgiving and all your deeds so do ye as ye find it in the Gospel of our Lord.

Obey this teaching and repent of your disobedience.

Read Matthew 6. Pray the Lord's Prayer three times and The Jesus Prayer without ceasing.

Day 16

Dadiche 16:1 Be watchful for your life; let your lamps not be quenched and your loins not ungirdled, but be ye ready; for ye know not the hour the hour in which our Lord cometh.

Dadiche 16:2 And ye shall gather yourselves together frequently, seeking what is fitting for your souls; for the whole time of your faith shall not profit you, if ye be not perfected at the last season.

Dadiche 16:3 For in the last days the false prophets and corrupters shall be multiplied, and the sheep shall be turned into wolves, and love shall be turned into hate.

Dadiche 16:4 For as lawlessness increaseth, they shall hate one another and shall persecute and betray. And then the world-deceiver shall appear as a son of God; and shall work signs and wonders, and the earth shall be delivered into his hands; and he shall do unholy things, which have never been since the world began.

Dadiche 16:5 Then all created mankind shall come to the fire of testing, and many shall be offended and perish; but they that endure in their faith shall be saved by the Curse Himself.

Dadiche 16:6 And then shall the signs of the truth appear; first a sign of a rift in the heaven, then a sign of a voice of a trumpet, and thirdly a resurrection of the dead.

Dadiche 16:7 Yet not of all, but as it was said The Lord shall come and all His saints with Him.

Dadiche 16:8 Then shall the world see the Lord coming upon the clouds of heaven.[4]

---

[4] http://housechurch.org/miscellaneous/didiche.html

Obey this teaching and repent of your disobedience.

Read Matthew 6. Pray the Lord's Prayer three times and The Jesus Prayer without ceasing.

Day 17

For these remaining days, I encourage you to implement these truths that I have adapted from *The 77 Irrefutable Truths of Prayer*[5] as you continue your training and equipping as a soldier who is a prayer warrior for Jesus Christ, all the time. **Pray to start and end your Day with God.**

> *Evening and morning and at noon I will pray,*
> *and cry aloud,*
> *And He shall hear my voice.*
> *-Psalm 55:17*

Start with prayer. *It's called proactive prayer.* If you begin today with a negative, self-centered, problem-driven focus, then your day's spiritual forecast reads:

> *Cloudy*
> *Storms Ahead*
> *Lightning Alert*
> *Prepare for a Shock!*

Honestly, to begin the day talking to anyone except God gives you their perspective instead of His; their problems instead of

---

[5] Keefauver, Larry & Judi. *Seventy-Seven Irrefutable Truths of Prayer* Bridge-Logos, 2003.

His; and their direction instead of His. Focus your *day-starting* prayer on God, not on things that you want or that distract you.

First-thought, first-talk, first-emotion prayer points you in the right direction and keeps you the head not the tail, the first and not the last, and the lender instead of the borrower. "The LORD WILL OPEN TO YOU HIS GOOD TREASURE, THE HEAVENS, TO GIVE THE RAIN TO YOUR LAND IN ITS SEASON, AND TO BLESS ALL THE WORK OF YOUR HAND. YOU SHALL LEND TO MANY NATIONS, BUT YOU SHALL NOT BORROW. AND THE LORD WILL MAKE YOU THE HEAD AND NOT THE TAIL; YOU SHALL BE ABOVE ONLY, AND NOT BE BENEATH, IF YOU HEED THE COMMANDMENTS OF THE LORD YOUR GOD, WHICH I COMMAND YOU TODAY, AND ARE CAREFUL TO OBSERVE *them.*" (Deut. 28:12-13).

End with prayer. Your *day-ending* prayer isn't a mopping up action. It's thanksgiving, praise-proclaiming time celebrating all that God did with, through, and in spite of you.

Starting your day without prayer guarantees a day ending with tears, sorrow and distress. Starting your day with prayer ensures ending your day with eyes opened to new miracles, greater glory, and incredible signs.

Think of it this way. Starting your day with prayer is like putting on glasses and seeing clearly both the visible and invisible. Without prayer, your day becomes like uncorrected vision so that you move ahead in a blurry, foggy haze not knowing when you'll stumble next.

Beginning prayer and ending prayer become the bookends for a day filled with dairies of divine communion.

God, I begin my day with You.
Direct my steps.
Unknot my emotions.

Clear my head.
Tune my Spirit to hear clearly the sounds of heaven.
Amen.

God, I end this day with You,
thankful for your provision and protection,
exulting in Your miracles,
excited by Your leading,
and rejoicing in Your forgiveness.
Repenting of my sins, I ask You to
refresh my spirit,
rest my body,
renew my mind,
and restore my relationships.
Amen.

Day 18

Pray the Jesus way.
In this manner, therefore, pray:
Our Father in heaven,
Hallowed be Your name.
–Matthew 6:9

Jesus taught us the way of prayer. The prayer He gave to his disciples models for us the basic elements of our every conversation with the Father.

Larry Lea pointed to each of these elements as starting with "P." I have adapted these as follows:

Papa. Jesus calls God, "Abba." He is our Father, our Papa, who loves and cares for us. *Our Father in heaven.*

Proclamation. We cry "Holy" with the angels in praise and honor to glorify God the King. His name is holy. To all flesh, we proclaim the name of the Lord. *Hallowed be Your name.*

Providence. As King, God has established His providence over all creation. Through habitual grace, God sustains His Kingdom as the rain falls on the just and the unjust. *Your kingdom come, Your will be done on earth as it is in heaven.*

Provision. God takes care of us. He alone is our source. Not our jobs, our spouse, our saving, or our strength can be our source. God alone provides. *Give us this day our daily bread.*

Pardon. God alone forgives sin. Through the shed blood of Jesus, God cleanses us from iniquity. Confessing our sins, He is faithful and just to forgive us (1 John 1:9). Receiving forgiveness arises not from our merit but from our willingness to forgive. Unforgiveness hardens our hearts to receiving His forgiveness. *Forgive us our debts, as we forgive our debtors.*

Protection. No weapon formed against us will prosper. Attacks may come from every side but God is our sure defense and strong tower. Under the shadow of His outstretched wings we abide and find refuge (Psalm 91). *And lead us not into temptation, but deliver us from the evil one.*

Power and Praise. No power can annul the purposes of God. No device of the enemy can thwart His good plans to prosper us. God inhabits our praise and conquers every foe. *For yours is the kingdom, and the power, and the glory forever. Amen.*

«

Our Father in heaven, Hallowed be Your name.
Your kingdom come. Your will be done
On earth as it is in heaven.
Give us this day our daily bread.
And forgive us our debts,
As we forgive our debtors.
And do not lead us into temptation,
But deliver us from the evil one.
For Yours is the kingdom and the power
and the glory forever. Amen.

Day 19

Pray with vigilance.

Continue earnestly in prayer,
being vigilant in it with thanksgiving.
–Colossians 4:2

The vigilant keep watch. Become a watchman on the tower with your prayers, as God said to Ezekiel, "I have made you a watchman" (Ezek. 3:17).

Watch for the enemy. As the watchman stands guard on the wall, he spies the enemy coming from afar. Sounding the alarm, the watchman alerts the city to a coming attack. Remember to pray for the Lord to guard the city or you will watch vainly in prayer (Psalm 127:1). Be watchful in prayer lest the devil seek you out and devour you (1 Peter 5:8).

Watch for the coming of the Lord. The watchman sees the sword of the Lord approaching (Ezek. 33). He proclaims the coming of the Day of the Lord. Ever vigilant and ready, the watchman in prayer knows the voice of the Lord and the sound of His approach.

Vigilant prayer prophesies.

Vigilant prayer is the prayer of the seer. "For thus has the Lord said to me: 'Go, set a watchman, Let him declare what he sees'" (Isa. 21:6).

Vigilant prayer births that which is seen prophetically. Elijah assumed a position of birthing and saw by the prayer of faith the rain that was coming.

> *And Elijah went up to the top of Carmel; then he bowed down on the ground, and put his face between his knees, and said to his servant, "Go up now, look toward the sea." So he went up and looked, and said, "There is nothing." And seven times he said, "Go again." Then it came to pass the seventh time, that he said, "There is a cloud, as small as a man's hand, rising out of the sea!"* (1 Kings 18:42-44)

Vigilant prayer never gives up, never quits, and never abandons the post. As long as the watch requires, the watchman alertly prays. Slumber tempts but cannot prevail. Fatigue weakens but cannot overcome. Impatience threatens but cannot erode the patient assurance and confident hope that steels the watchman in vigilant prayer.

Almighty God,
Keep me awake in prayer.
Let sleeplessness be my spiritual state.

*As I pray,
permit me to see the coming attacks,
that I may alert my household,
and prepare to stand firm.
As I watch with vigilance,
reveal to me your coming rain,
that I might prophesy your refreshing.
Amen.*

Day 20

Pray before the battle.

*When Your people go out to battle against their enemy, wherever You send them, and when they pray to the LORD toward the city which You have chosen and the temple which I have built for Your name,
then hear in heaven their prayer and their supplication, and maintain their cause.*
–1 Kings 8:44-45

Before Israel went into battle, Solomon prayed entreating God for victory.

Before battling Jericho, the people of Israel marched, blew the trumpets and then shouted to the Lord. Before the battle of Jericho, God revealed to Joshua that the city was already his—the battle was already won! (Read Joshua 6:1-2)

Before battling the Midianites, Gideon spoke with the Lord, built an altar of worship, and obeyed what God told him.

Before battling Goliath, David declared that the battle belonged to the Lord.

Before facing the Assyrians in battle, King Hezekiah prayed unto the Lord and the battle was won by God before any stone was cast or weapon thrown.

Before facing the Ammonites and Moabites in battle, King Jehoshaphat and the people bowed before God, praised Him and stood still to see the salvation of the Lord (2 Chron. 20).

Before facing the battle of Golgotha and triumphing over the enemies of death and sin on the cross, Jesus prayed in Gethsemane, "Thy will not mine be done."

Here's the prayer key we need to understand: *proactive prayer anticipates both the coming battle and the victory that God has already won.*

Be proactive not reactive. Our tendency in prayer is to be reactive instead of proactive. In the midst of the battle when the tide turns against us, then we cry out, "Oh God, save me." Our problem is that we have entered the battle in our own strength and fought with our own weapons instead of fighting the battle God's way with His weapons. "For the weapons of our warfare are not carnal but mighty in God for pulling down strongholds" (2 Cor. 10:4).

Pray before the battle. Get the mind of the Lord for the battle. Ask God to maintain His cause and purpose for the battle. Rest in the truth that the battle is never against flesh and blood (Eph. 6). Remember that the enemy is never the other person but always the father of lies who seeks to steal, kill and destroy (John 10:10).

Spirit of God,
Capture my attention before any battle.
Keep my focus on you not the enemy.
Reveal to me the device and wiles of the enemy.
Release your power and might to win the victory.
I praise you in advance for the victory! Amen.

Day 21

Abide patiently in prayer.
Continuing steadfastly in prayer.
–Romans 12:12

This phrase in the Greek implies that we need to dwell, abide, even to rest in prayer. Urgent prayer isn't about needing an answer *now*. Praying with urgency has to do with being urgent to get alone with God, to withdraw immediately into His presence, to rush to meet with Him *now*.

Once there, once we enter the secret place under the shadow of His wings (Ps. 91), we can rest, abide, and wait patiently and confidently in Him. Before we prayed, His answer was there. Before we came, He was waiting for us. Before we asked, He had prepared a table, yes even a feast for us.

Jesus stands at the door of our hearts (Rev. 3:20) and knocks. We are the ones resisting, not God. We are the ones restless, not God.

Abiding patiently in prayer means...

Always keeping our heart's door open to Jesus.

Always trusting that His way and timing are best.

Always resting in Him instead of rushing around trying to find Him.

Always dwelling at His place instead of maintaining our place.

Always waiting for Him instead of impatiently wanting from Him.

Always listening without interrupting.

Prayer isn't talking with God on our terms; prayer listens to God abiding by His terms. When we feel God hasn't answered, it's only a feeling. Feelings are always real but not always reality.

The truth is that God always answers, but we must patiently wait for His timing and way. I want an answer in my time. He gives His answer in His time.

Abiding patiently in prayer is hard until we finally surrender our will to His, our way to His, and our wants to His.

God,
Grant me the patience to wait for Your answer,
instead of lobbying incessantly for my answer.
Grant me the desire to unlock the door
and throw away the key,
So that You always have free access to my soul.
Amen.

Day 22

Pray with fasting to see deliverance.
*However, this kind does not go out
except by prayer and fasting.*
–Matthew 17:21

Prayer applies God's power and healing to the situation. Fasting applies our attention and focus.

Pray centers our mind on God. Fasting takes our minds off of our needs and fixes our minds on His needs.

Prayer surrenders wants. Fasting lets go of wants and cries out for what God desires.

Prayer seeks, knocks and asks. Fasting receives, opens and answers. In fasting, I deny myself physical food in order to receive spiritual food, i.e. the bread of life. In fasting, I unlock the inner chambers of my heart to open myself to all the light and revelation God wants me to have. In fasting, I cease asking God questions, and I begin answering God's inquiries of me.

In prayer, I connect with God. Prayer is like plugging in a power cord. Fasting, like turning on the switch, releases the power to change me and those around me.

Prayer takes me up from earth to heaven; fasting brings heaven to earth. Fasting empties me of earth so that heaven might fill me.

Prayer vacates my soul of self so that fasting can produce such hunger and thirst for God that nothing but God can satisfy.

Prayer digs the well. Fasting keeps the well cleaned out.

> *Lord,*
> *give me a willingness to pray and fast,*
> *a humility to receive what that will bring,*
> *and obedience to do whatever it takes*
> *to follow Your Spirit.*
> *Amen.*

Day 23

Obey to pray.

One who turns away his ear from hearing the law,
Even his prayer is an abomination.
–Proverbs 28:9

The only way to pray when disobeying is to repent. Repentance requires not only contrition but also the conviction to stop sinning and start doing what's right.

Too often we expect God to hear and answer our prayers when we come to him with dirty hands and hearts. Clean up your act through repentance and obedience. "Therefore, having these promises, beloved, let us cleanse ourselves from all filthiness of the flesh and spirit, perfecting holiness in the fear of God" (2 Cor. 7:1).

Prayer cannot excuse or nullify the effects of disobedience. Prayer turns the heart away from disobedience to weeping contrition before God. Prayer coupled with disobedience adds insult to injury before God.

Want a powerful prayer life? **Obey God.** A key to effective prayer is your obedience. Here's the sequence of powerful pray:

Trust ➜ Obedience ➜ Prayer ➜ Power

Jesus,
teach me to trust and obey,
So that when I pray,
Your power will flow.
Amen.

Day 24

Stay the watch.

"Watch and pray, lest you enter into temptation. The spirit indeed is willing, but the flesh is weak."
–Matthew 26:41

Stay the watch. Don't retire before your watch is over and you've been relieved. Be alert. It's never too late and you should never be too tired to pray.

When the flesh is weak, don't try to stay the watch alone. Get help and support.

- Pray with a prayer partner.
- Ask the Spirit to help you pray.
- Pray the Word of God.
- Pray in the Spirit.
- Gather with other saints to worship and prayer.
- Pray in different positions of prayer—standing, kneeling, lying prostrate, walking, lifting holy hands and bowing in prayer.
- Fast and pray.
- Worship, sing, praise and shout your prayer.

Scripture commands us to rest. Pray when you're rested. Take care of the temple of your body. Watching and praying gives you the strength to resist temptation.

*God,
empower me to stay the watch.
Amen.*

Day 25

Pray for mercy.
God, be merciful to me a sinner!
–Luke 18:13

In prayer all pretense melts away, leaving us to face the stark reality of who we are, not who we would like to be.

In prayer our greatest needs are exposed along with our greatest sins.

In prayer we cry out for mercy because nothing else can be uttered.

In prayer we desperately seek what we cannot do for ourselves—forgiveness.

In prayer we don't care who listens or what they think of us. All that matters is what God thinks of us.

In prayer God's mercy reminds me of my complete inability to forgive myself much less others.

In prayer I confess that until I receive mercy, I have nothing else to pray.

Praying this mercy prayer offends the self-righteous. Not praying it leaves me mired in offense.

Lord,
be merciful to me, a sinner.
Amen.

Day 26

Pray for deliverance.

For I know that this will turn out for my deliverance through
Your prayer
and the supply of the Spirit of Jesus Christ.
–Philippians 1:19

The gospel declares that Jesus saves, heals, and delivers us. Jesus saves us from sin and for eternal life with Him. Jesus heals us physically and emotionally. Jesus delivers us from the bondages of past sin, curses, strongholds, diseases, and failures.

When others are bound by addictions, abuse, abandonment, and afflictions, apply the prescription that God provides—prayer. Go to the Great Physician and ask Him to deliver them.

No ritual or formula is needed. Jesus provided us with the example. He simply spoke the word of deliverance and people were set free. Pray like this: "Come out of them, in Jesus' name."

People are delivered by prayer and the supply of the Spirit of Jesus Christ. Through prayer become the instrument of the Spirit's delivering power in the lives of others.

Spirit of God,
pray through me to deliver others,
breaking every yoke of bondage
and declaring the liberty of Christ Jesus.
Amen.

Day 27

Intercede with Christ in the secret place.

Who is he who condemns? It is Christ who died, and furthermore is also risen,
who is even at the right hand of God, who also makes intercession for us.
–Romans 8:34

Where is the secret place of prayer? It's not a physical place even though you may have your favorite retreat or closet of prayer.

Jesus instructs, "But you, when you pray, go into your room, and when you have shut your door, pray to your Father who is in the **secret place;** and your Father who sees in secret will reward you openly" (Matt. 6:6).

That secret place of prayer is in the **heavenly places**: "and raised us up together, and made us sit together in the heavenly places in Christ Jesus" (Eph. 2:6).

That secret place of prayer is in the **shadow of the Almighty:** "He who dwells in the secret place of the Most High shall abide under the shadow of the Almighty" (Ps. 91:1).

In that secret place of prayer, we can hide in the **presence of God:** "You shall hide them in the secret place of Your presence" (Ps. 31:20).

No matter how weak we feel or shaken our lives may become as we reel under pressures and stress, in the secret place **we stand on the Rock**:

In the secret place of His tabernacle
He shall hide me;
He shall set me high upon a rock.
(Ps. 27:5)

In that secret place, **we pray with Christ** as He intercedes for us. We pray His will for us. We listen to His words and heart and pray what He prays.

For no earthly reason we may find ourselves praying for a city, a nation, a person, or a situation unknown to us in the natural. How does that happen? God has raised us into the heavenly places. There we hear the prayer of Jesus. By His Spirit, we enter into the secret place of prayer.

The prayer of the secret place releases miracles we may never know of until we step into eternal life. The prayer of the secret place provides provision for which others are desperate. The prayer of the secret place releases healing into the sick lives of those we have never met.

The prayer of the secret place moves beyond what we know into the revelation of what He knows. It is often the inexpressible prayer of travail and moaning given to us by the Spirit.

The prayer of the secret place moves us from praying to Christ into praying with Christ. It takes us from doing our work into doing His work: "Most assuredly, I say to you, he who believes in Me, the works that I do he will do also; and greater works than these he will do, because I go to My Father. And whatever you ask in My name, that I will do, that the Father may be glorified in the Son. 14 If you ask anything in My name, I will do it" (John 14:12-14).

Father,
hide me in your secret place.
Jesus,
let me hear your intercession
that I may know how to pray.
Holy Spirit,
intercede through me to accomplish
Your eternal will.
Amen.

Day 28

Pray the word.
Remember, I pray, the word that You commanded Your servant Moses
–Nehemiah 1:8

Praying God's Word doesn't remind God of what He needs to do. Praying God's Word reminds us of His promises so that we might release the power of His Word into this hour for His will and glory to be revealed.

In the following pages of action-truths, I am encouraging you to pray the Word. Space is provided for you to pray. Insert your name and/or the names of others.

I am not commenting on the scriptures. Simply pray them. Take time to pray out loud. Pray for everyone whom God places on your heart.

Praying God's Word speaks that promise or truth of God into this moment of time and space.

Praying God's Word births promise into the *now* of our lives. Praying God's Word declares His will for us. Praying God's Word takes prayer from the realm of my thoughts into His thoughts.

Pray the word! Begin by praying Psalm 119:10-16:

With my whole heart I have sought You;
Oh, let me not wander from Your commandments!
Your word I have hidden in my heart,
That I might not sin against You!
Blessed are You, O LORD!
Teach me Your statutes!
With my lips I have declared
All the judgments of Your mouth.
I have rejoiced in the way of Your testimonies,
As much as in all riches.
I will meditate on Your precepts,
And contemplate Your ways.
I will delight myself in Your statutes;
I will not forget Your word.
Amen.

Day 29

Confess your sin and the sins of others.
Now while I was speaking, praying, and confessing my sin
and the sin of my people Israel,
and presenting my supplication before the LORD my God for
the holy mountain of my God.
–Daniel 9:20

Isn't it enough that I confess my own sins? Why is it that I must also confess the sins of others?

Because in prayer we stand in the gap for others. Not only do our personal sins bind us; the corporate sins of our family, community, church and nation hinder us.

When you confess sin, begin with your own personal transgressions, but don't stop there. Be cleansed of the corporate sins of those around you. Personal confession frees you to move around in your own territory, but what a small arena of power and influence that may be.

Corporate confession frees you to move into realms of intercession far beyond your personal sphere of influence. It moves you into warring against principalities and powers:

"Finally, my brethren, be strong in the Lord and in the power of His might. Put on the whole armor of God, that you may be able to stand against the wiles of the devil. For we do not wrestle against flesh and blood, but against principalities, against powers, against the rulers of the darkness of this age, against spiritual hosts of wickedness in the heavenly places" (Eph. 6:10-12).

Almighty God,
I confess my sins and the sins of my family,
my church,
my community,
my nation.
I stand firm against the principalities and powers that would
seek to bind us up
and render us powerless.
I boldly put on the armor of God,
standing firm against the evil one,
praying for all the saints,
declaring victory over every evil in Jesus' name.
Amen.

Day 30

Pray for wisdom.

*If any of you lacks wisdom, let him ask of God,
who gives to all liberally and without reproach,
and it will be given to him.*
—James 1:5

Wisdom sees everything from God's perspective. My perspective can only see what's visible and what's locked in time and space. But from God's perspective I can see myself and others as He sees us. From God's perspective I can take the long look into what's best for both now and the future.

Wisdom lines up knowledge and understanding so that I may walk a straight path in God's ways.

Knowledge is the revelation of His truth through His Word that keeps us from sin and directs us in the paths of righteousness for His name's sake. Knowledge brings me into an intimacy with Him so that I may hear his voice before I take the next step in my spiritual walk.

Understanding applies correctly what God has revealed to me. With understanding I can do the new thing that God has shown me without fear of failure.

God's Word declares, "For the LORD gives wisdom; From His mouth come knowledge and understanding" (Prov. 2:6). Want God's perspective? Pray for wisdom.

*Lord God,
Give me wisdom that I may see what You see.
Give me knowledge that I may know You.
Give me understanding that I may do
Your will.
Amen.*

Praying with the Commander in Chief

Serving in the military, I was always aware that my ultimate senior officer was the Commander in Chief...the President of the United States. I want to share with you some of the prayers of these warriors, these ultimate soldiers sworn to protect this nation that confesses, "In God We Trust."

The prayers are merely a sampling from our Presidents. Use these prayers to encourage and equip your own prayer life as a soldier of Jesus Christ.

"Almighty God, We make our earnest prayer that Thou wilt keep the United States in Thy holy protection: that Thou wilt incline the hearts of the citizens to cultivate a spirit of subordination and obedience to government, and entertain a brotherly affection and love for one another and for their fellow citizens of the United States at large. And finally that Thou wilt most graciously be pleased to dispose us all to do justice, to love mercy, and to demean ourselves with that charity, humility, and pacific temper of mind which were the characteristics of the Divine Author of our blessed religion, and without a humble imitation of whose example in these things we can never hope to be a happy nation. Grant our supplication, we beseech Thee, through Jesus Christ our Lord. Amen."

— A DAILY PRAYER OF GEORGE WASHINGTON

"Almighty God,

Who has given us this good land for our heritage; We humbly beseech Thee that we may always prove ourselves a people mindful of Thy favor and glad to do Thy will. Bless our land with honorable ministry, sound learning, and pure manners. Save us from violence, discord, and confusion, from pride and arrogance, and from every evil way. Defend our liberties, and fashion into one united people, the multitude brought hither out of many kindreds and tongues. Endow with Thy spirit of wisdom those whom in Thy Name we entrust the authority of government, that there may be justice and peace at home, and that through obedience to Thy law, we may show forth Thy praise among the nations of the earth. In time of prosperity fill our hearts with thankfulness, and in the Day of trouble, suffer not our trust in Thee to fail; all of which we ask through Jesus Christ our Lord. Amen."

>—MARCH 4, 1805, A NATIONAL PRAYER
> FOR PEACE—Thomas Jefferson

"Tis my fervent prayer to that Almighty Being that He will so overrule all my intentions and actions and inspire the hearts of my fellow citizens that we may be preserved from dangers of all kinds and continue forever a united, happy people."

>—MARCH 4, 1833—Andrew Jackson

"ToDay I leave you; I go to assume a task more difficult than that which devolved upon General Washington. Unless the great God who assisted him, shall be with and aid me, I must fail. But if the same omniscient mind, and the same Almighty arm that directed and protected him, shall guide and support me, I shall not fail, I shall succeed.

Let us all pray that the God of our fathers may not forsake us now. To Him I commend you all–permit me to ask that with equal sincerity and faith, you all will invoke His wisdom and guidance for me.

With these few words I must leave you–for how long I know not. Friends, one and all, I must now bid you an affectionate farewell."

—FEBRUARY 12, 1861 LINCOLN'S DEPARTURE FOR WASHINGTON, DC—
Abraham Lincoln

"O Lord our Heavenly Father, who has safely brought us to the beginning of this day; defend us in the same with Thy Almighty power. Grant that we may not fall into any kind of danger and keep us from evil. May all our doings be ordered by Thy governance so that all we do may be righteous in Thy sight. Amen"

—Rutherford Hayes

"I pray God I may be given the wisdom and prudence to do my duty in the true spirit of this great people."

—2ND INAUGURAL ADDRESS, MARCH 5, 1917—Woodrow Wilson

"Almighty God: Our sons, pride of our Nation, this Day have set upon a mighty endeavor, a struggle to preserve our Republic, our religion, and our civilization, and to set free a suffering humanity.

Lead them straight and true; give strength to their arms, stoutness to their hearts, steadfastness in their faith.

They will need Thy blessings. Their road will be long and hard. For the enemy is strong. He may hurl back our forces. Success may not come with rushing speed, but we shall return again and again; and we know that by Thy grace, and by the righteousness of our cause, our sons will triumph.

They will be sore tried, by night and by day, without rest-until the victory is won. The darkness will be rent by noise and flame. Men's souls will be shaken with the violences of war.

And, O Lord, give us Faith. Give us Faith in Thee; Faith in our sons; Faith in each other; Faith in our united crusade. Let not the keenness of our spirit ever be dulled. Let not the impacts of temporary events, of temporal matters of but fleeting moment let not these deter us in our unconquerable purpose.

With Thy blessing, we shall prevail over the unholy forces of our enemy. Help us to conquer the apostles of greed and racial arrogancies. Lead us to the saving of our country, and with our sister Nations into a world unity that will spell a sure peace a peace invulnerable to the schemings of unworthy men. And a peace that will let all of men live in freedom, reaping the just rewards of their honest toil.

Thy will be done, Almighty God. Amen."

—Prayer on D-Day, June 6, 1944—
Franklin Roosevelt

"Oh! Almighty and Everlasting God, Creator of Heaven, Earth and the Universe, help me to be, to think, to act what is right, because it is right; make me truthful, honest and honorable in all things; make me intellectually honest for the sake of right and honor and without thought of reward to me. Give me the ability to be charitable, forgiving and patient with my fellowmen–help me to understand their motives and their shortcoming–even as Thou understandest mine! Amen, Amen, Amen."

—Harry Truman August 15, 1950

"Almighty God, as we stand here, at this moment, my future associates in the executive branch of the government join me in beseeching that Thou will make full and complete our dedication to the service of the people in this throng and their fellow citizens everywhere. Give us, we pray, the power to discern clearly right from wrong and allow all our works and actions to be governed thereby and by the laws of the land. Especially we pray that our concerns shall be for all the people, regardless of station, race, or calling. May cooperation be permitted and be the mutual aim of those who, under the concept of our Constitution, hold to differing political beliefs, so that all may work for the good of our beloved country and for Thy glory. Amen."

> —2ND INAUGURAL ADDRESS,
> JAN. 21, 1957—Dwight Eisenhower

"May God guide this wonderful country, its people, and those they have chosen to lead them. May our third century be illuminated by liberty and blessed with brotherhood, so that we and all who come after us may be the humble servants of thy peace. Amen."

> —STATE OF THE UNION ADDRESS,
> JAN. 12, 1977—Gerald Ford

"Heavenly Father, we bow our heads and thank you for Your love. Accept our thanks for the peace that yields this Day and the shared faith that makes its continuance likely. Make us strong to do Your work, willing to heed and hear Your will, and write on our hearts these words: 'Use power to help people.' For we are given power not to advance our own purposes, nor to make a great show in the world, nor a name. There is but one just use of power, and it is to serve people. Help us to remember it, Lord, Amen."

>—A PROCLAMATION–NATIONAL Day OF PRAYER 1990 BY GEORGE BUSH, PRESIDENT OF THE UNITED STATES OF AMERICA—George H. Bush

"I pray that our leaders will always act with humility and generosity. I pray that my failings are forgiven. I pray that we will uphold our obligation to be good stewards of God's creation - this beautiful planet. I pray that we will see every single child as our own, each worthy of our love and of our compassion. And I pray we answer Scripture's call to lift up the vulnerable, and to stand up for justice, and ensure that every human being lives in dignity."

>—National Prayer Breakfast, Feb 4, 2016— Barack Obama

ABOUT THE AUTHOR

Pastor Leslie Gomez was born in Brooklyn, New York. He retired from the Marines after serving for twenty-two years and now works at Gulfstream Aerospace. He and his wife of twenty-five years have three daughters, and they live in Bluffton S.C., Atlanta Georgia and Dallas Texas. He graduated from Liberty University with a BA in Religion in 2012. He now pastors Iglesia Cristiana Unida, a bilingual church in South Carolina.

CPSIA information can be obtained
at www.ICGtesting.com
Printed in the USA
LVHW051222251119
638400LV00004B/619/P